THE PELICAN SHAKESPEARE
GENERAL EDITORS

STEPHEN ORGEL
A. R. BRAUNMULLER

The Comedy of Errors

An eighteenth-century *Comedy of Errors:*
"Mr. Dunstal in the Character of the Syracusan Dromio,"
from Bell's Shakespeare, 1776

William Shakespeare

The Comedy of Errors

EDITED BY FRANCES E. DOLAN

PENGUIN BOOKS

PENGUIN BOOKS
Published by the Penguin Group
Penguin Group (USA) Inc., 375 Hudson Street, New York, New York 10014, U.S.A.
Penguin Group (Canada), 90 Eglinton Avenue East, Suite 700, Toronto,
Ontario, Canada M4P 2Y3 (a division of Pearson Penguin Canada Inc.)
Penguin Books Ltd, 80 Strand, London WC2R 0RL, England
Penguin Ireland, 25 St Stephen's Green, Dublin 2, Ireland (a division of Penguin Books Ltd)
Penguin Group (Australia), 250 Camberwell Road, Camberwell,
Victoria 3124, Australia (a division of Pearson Australia Group Pty Ltd)
Penguin Books India Pvt Ltd, 11 Community Centre, Panchsheel Park, New Delhi – 110 017, India
Penguin Group (NZ), cnr Airborne and Rosedale Roads,
Albany, Auckland 1310, New Zealand (a division of Pearson New Zealand Ltd)
Penguin Books (South Africa) (Pty) Ltd, 24 Sturdee Avenue,
Rosebank, Johannesburg 2196, South Africa

Penguin Books Ltd, Registered Offices: 80 Strand, London WC2R 0RL, England

The Comedy of Errors edited by Paul A. Jorgensen published in
the United States of America in Penguin Books 1964
Revised edition published 1972
This new edition edited by Frances E. Dolan published 1999

20 19 18 17 16 15 14 13 12 11

Copyright © Penguin Books Inc., 1964, 1972
Copyright © Penguin Putnam Inc., 1999
All rights reserved

ISBN 0-14-07.1474-X

Printed in the United States of America
Set in Garamond
Designed by Virginia Norey

Except in the United States of America, this book is sold subject to the condition
that it shall not, by way of trade or otherwise, be lent, resold, hired out, or otherwise
circulated without the publisher's prior consent in any form of binding or cover other
than that in which it is published and without a similar condition including
this condition being imposed on the subsequent purchaser.

The scanning, uploading and distribution of this book via the Internet or via any
other means without the permission of the publisher is illegal and punishable by law.
Please purchase only authorized electronic editions, and do not participate in or encourage
electronic piracy of copyrighted materials. Your support of the author's rights is appreciated.

Contents

Publisher's Note   vii

The Theatrical World   ix

The Texts of Shakespeare   xxv

Introduction   xxxi

Note on the Text   xliii

The Comedy of Errors   1

Publisher's Note

IT IS ALMOST half a century since the first volumes of the Pelican Shakespeare appeared under the general editorship of Alfred Harbage. The fact that a new edition, rather than simply a revision, has been undertaken reflects the profound changes textual and critical studies of Shakespeare have undergone in the past twenty years. For the new Pelican series, the texts of the plays and poems have been thoroughly revised in accordance with recent scholarship, and in some cases have been entirely reedited. New introductions and notes have been provided in all the volumes. But the new Shakespeare is also designed as a successor to the original series; the previous editions have been taken into account, and the advice of the previous editors has been solicited where it was feasible to do so.

Certain textual features of the new Pelican Shakespeare should be particularly noted. All lines are numbered that contain a word, phrase, or allusion explained in the glossarial notes. In addition, for convenience, every tenth line is also numbered, in italics when no annotation is indicated. The intrusive and often inaccurate place headings inserted by early editors are omitted (as is becoming standard practice), but for the convenience of those who miss them, an indication of locale now appears as the first item in the annotation of each scene.

In the interest of both elegance and utility, each speech prefix is set in a separate line when the speaker's lines are in verse, except when those words form the second half of a verse line. Thus the verse form of the speech is kept visually intact. What is printed as verse and what is printed as prose has, in general, the authority of the original texts. Departures from the original texts in this regard have only the authority of editorial tradition and the judgment of the Pelican editors; and, in a few instances, are admittedly arbitrary.

The Theatrical World

ECONOMIC REALITIES determined the theatrical world in which Shakespeare's plays were written, performed, and received. For centuries in England, the primary theatrical tradition was nonprofessional. Craft guilds (or "mysteries") provided religious drama – mystery plays – as part of the celebration of religious and civic festivals, and schools and universities staged classical and neoclassical drama in both Latin and English as part of their curricula. In these forms, drama was established and socially acceptable. Professional theater, in contrast, existed on the margins of society. The acting companies were itinerant; playhouses could be any available space – the great halls of the aristocracy, town squares, civic halls, inn yards, fair booths, or open fields – and income was sporadic, dependent on the passing of the hat or on the bounty of local patrons. The actors, moreover, were considered little better than vagabonds, constantly in danger of arrest or expulsion.

In the late 1560s and 1570s, however, English professional theater began to gain respectability. Wealthy aristocrats fond of drama – the Lord Admiral, for example, or the Lord Chamberlain – took acting companies under their protection so that the players technically became members of their households and were no longer subject to arrest as homeless or masterless men. Permanent theaters were first built at this time as well, allowing the companies to control and charge for entry to their performances.

Shakespeare's livelihood, and the stunning artistic explosion in which he participated, depended on pragmatic and architectural effort. Professional theater requires ways to restrict access to its offerings; if it does not, and admission fees cannot be charged, the actors do not get paid, the costumes go to a pawnbroker, and there is no such thing as a professional, ongoing theatrical tradition. The answer to that economic need arrived in the late 1560s and 1570s with the creation of the so-called public or amphitheater playhouse. Recent discoveries indicate that the precursor of the Globe playhouse in London (where Shakespeare's mature plays were presented) and the Rose theater (which presented Christopher Marlowe's plays and some of Shakespeare's earliest ones) was the Red Lion theater of 1567. Archaeological studies of the foundations of the Rose and Globe theaters have revealed that the open-air theater of the 1590s and later was probably a polygonal building with fourteen to twenty or twenty-four sides, multistoried, from 75 to 100 feet in diameter, with a raised, partly covered "thrust" stage that projected into a group of standing patrons, or "groundlings," and a covered gallery, seating up to 2,500 or more (very crowded) spectators.

These theaters might have been about half full on any given day, though the audiences were larger on holidays or when a play was advertised, as old and new were, through printed playbills posted around London. The metropolitan area's late-Tudor, early-Stuart population (circa 1590-1620) has been estimated at about 150,000-250,000. It has been supposed that in the mid-1590s there were about 15,000 spectators per week at the public theaters; thus, as many as 10 percent of the local population went to the theater regularly. Consequently, the theaters' repertories – the plays available for this experienced and frequent audience – had to change often: in the month between September 15 and October 15, 1595, for instance, the Lord Admiral's Men performed twenty-eight times in eighteen different plays.

Since natural light illuminated the amphitheaters' stages, performances began between noon and two o'clock and ran without a break for two or three hours. They often concluded with a jig, a fencing display, or some other nondramatic exhibition. Weather conditions determined the season for the amphitheaters: plays were performed every day (including Sundays, sometimes, to clerical dismay) except during Lent – the forty days before Easter – or periods of plague, or sometimes during the summer months when law courts were not in session and the most affluent members of the audience were not in London.

To a modern theatergoer, an amphitheater stage like that of the Rose or Globe would appear an unfamiliar mixture of plainness and elaborate decoration. Much of the structure was carved or painted, sometimes to imitate marble; elsewhere, as under the canopy projecting over the stage, to represent the stars and the zodiac. Appropriate painted canvas pictures (of Jerusalem, for example, if the play was set in that city) were apparently hung on the wall behind the acting area, and tragedies were accompanied by black hangings, presumably something like crepe festoons or bunting. Although these theaters did not employ what we would call scenery, early modern spectators saw numerous large props, such as the "bar" at which a prisoner stood during a trial, the "mossy bank" where lovers reclined, an arbor for amorous conversation, a chariot, gallows, tables, trees, beds, thrones, writing desks, and so forth. Audiences might learn a scene's location from a sign (reading "Athens," for example) carried across the stage (as in Bertolt Brecht's twentieth-century productions). Equally captivating (and equally irritating to the theater's enemies) were the rich costumes and personal props the actors used: the most valuable items in the surviving theatrical inventories are the swords, gowns, robes, crowns, and other items worn or carried by the performers.

Magic appealed to Shakespeare's audiences as much as it does to us today, and the theater exploited many deceptive and spectacular devices. A winch in the loft above the stage, called "the heavens," could lower and raise actors playing gods, goddesses, and other supernatural figures to and from the main acting area, just as one or more trapdoors permitted entrances and exits to and from the area, called "hell," beneath the stage. Actors wore elementary makeup such as wigs, false beards, and face paint, and they employed pig's bladders filled with animal blood to make wounds seem more real. They had rudimentary but effective ways of pretending to behead or hang a person. Supernumeraries (stagehands or actors not needed in a particular scene) could make thunder sounds (by shaking a metal sheet or rolling an iron ball down a chute) and show lightning (by blowing inflammable resin through tubes into a flame). Elaborate fireworks enhanced the effects of dragons flying through the air or imitated such celestial phenomena as comets, shooting stars, and multiple suns. Horses' hoofbeats, bells (located perhaps in the tower above the stage), trumpets and drums, clocks, cannon shots and gunshots, and the like were common sound effects. And the music of viols, cornets, oboes, and recorders was a regular feature of theatrical performances.

For two relatively brief spans, from the late 1570s to 1590 and from 1599 to 1614, the amphitheaters competed with the so-called private, or indoor, theaters, which originated as, or later represented themselves as, educational institutions training boys as singers for church services and court performances. These indoor theaters had two features that were distinct from the amphitheaters': their personnel and their playing spaces. The amphitheaters' adult companies included both adult men, who played the male roles, and boys, who played the female roles; the private, or indoor, theater companies, on the other hand, were entirely composed of boys aged about 8 to 16, who were, or could pretend to be, candidates for singers in a church or a royal boys' choir. (Until 1660, professional theatrical companies included no women.) The playing space would appear much more familiar to modern audiences than the long-vanished amphitheaters; the later indoor theaters were, in fact, the ancestors of the typical modern theater. They were enclosed spaces, usually rectangular, with the stage filling one end of the rectangle and the audience arrayed in seats or benches across (and sometimes lining) the building's longer axis. These spaces staged plays less frequently than the public theaters (perhaps only once a week) and held far fewer spectators than the amphitheaters: about 200–600, as opposed to 2,500 or more. Fewer patrons mean a smaller gross income, unless each pays more. Not surprisingly, then, private theaters charged higher prices than the amphitheaters, probably sixpence, as opposed to a penny for the cheapest entry.

Protected from the weather, the indoor theaters presented plays later in the day than the amphitheaters, and used artificial illumination – candles in sconces or candelabra. But candles melt, and need replacing, snuffing, and trimming, and these practical requirements may have been part of the reason the indoor theaters introduced breaks in the performance, the intermission so dear to the heart of theatergoers and to the pocketbooks of theater concessionaires ever since. Whether motivated by the need to tend to the candles or by the entrepreneurs' wishing to sell oranges and liquor, or both, the indoor theaters eventually established the modern convention of the non-continuous performance. In the early modern "private" theater, musical performances apparently filled the intermissions, which in Stuart theater jargon seem to have been called "acts."

At the end of the first decade of the seventeenth century, the distinction between public amphitheaters and private indoor companies ceased. For various cultural, political, and economic reasons, individual companies gained control of both the public, open-air theaters and the indoor ones, and companies mixing adult men and boys took over the formerly "private" theaters. Despite the death of the boys' companies and of their highly innovative theaters (for which such luminous playwrights as Ben Jonson, George Chapman, and John Marston wrote), their playing spaces and conventions had an immense impact on subsequent plays: not merely for the intervals (which stressed the artistic and architectonic importance of "acts"), but also because they introduced political and social satire as a popular dramatic ingredient, even in tragedy, and a wider range of actorly effects, encouraged by their more intimate playing spaces.

Even the briefest sketch of the Shakespearean theatrical world would be incomplete without some comment on the social and cultural dimensions of theaters and playing in the period. In an intensely hierarchical and status-conscious society, professional actors and their ventures had hardly any respectability; as we have indicated, to protect themselves against laws designed to curb vagabondage and the increase of masterless men, actors resorted to the near-fiction that they were the servants of noble masters, and wore their distinctive livery. Hence the company for which Shakespeare wrote in the 1590s called itself the Lord Chamberlain's Men and pretended that the public, money-getting performances were in fact rehearsals for private performances before that high court official. From 1598, the Privy Council had licensed theatrical companies, and after 1603, with the accession of King James I, the companies gained explicit royal protection, just as the Queen's Men had for a time under Queen Elizabeth. The Chamberlain's Men became the King's Men, and the other companies were patronized by the other members of the royal family.

These designations were legal fictions that half-concealed an important economic and social development, the evolution away from the theater's organization on the model of the guild, a self-regulating confraternity of individual artisans, into a proto-capitalist organization. Shakespeare's company became a joint-stock company, where persons who supplied capital and, in some cases, such as Shakespeare's, capital and talent, employed themselves and others in earning a return on that capital. This development meant that actors and theater companies were outside both the traditional guild structures, which required some form of civic or royal charter, and the feudal household organization of master-and-servant. This anomalous, maverick social and economic condition made theater companies practically unruly and potentially even dangerous; consequently, numerous official bodies – including the London metropolitan and ecclesiastical authorities as well as, occasionally, the royal court itself – tried, without much success, to control and even to disband them.

Public officials had good reason to want to close the theaters: they were attractive nuisances – they drew often riotous crowds, they were always noisy, and they could be politically offensive and socially insubordinate. Until the Civil War, however, anti-theatrical forces failed to shut down professional theater, for many reasons – limited surveillance and few police powers, tensions or outright hostilities among the agencies that sought to check or channel theatrical activity, and lack of clear policies for control. Another reason must have been the theaters' undeniable popularity. Curtailing any activity enjoyed by such a substantial percentage of the population was difficult, as various Roman emperors attempting to limit circuses had learned, and the Tudor-Stuart audience was not merely large, it was socially diverse and included women. The prevalence of public entertainment in this period has been underestimated. In fact, fairs, holidays, games, sporting events, the equivalent of modern parades, freak shows, and street exhibitions all abounded, but the theater was the most widely and frequently available entertainment to which people of every class had access. That fact helps account both for its quantity and for the fear and anger it aroused.

WILLIAM SHAKESPEARE OF
STRATFORD-UPON-AVON, GENTLEMAN

Many people have said that we know very little about William Shakespeare's life – pinheads and postcards are often mentioned as appropriately tiny surfaces on which to record the available information. More imaginatively and perhaps more correctly, Ralph Waldo Emerson wrote, "Shakespeare is the only biographer of Shakespeare. . . . So far from Shakespeare's being the least known, he is the one person in all modern history fully known to us."

In fact, we know more about Shakespeare's life than we do about almost any other English writer's of his era. His last will and testament (dated March 25, 1616) survives, as do numerous legal contracts and court documents involving Shakespeare as principal or witness, and parish records in Stratford and London. Shakespeare appears quite often in official records of King James's royal court, and of course Shakespeare's name appears on numerous title pages and in the written and recorded words of his literary contemporaries Robert Greene, Henry Chettle, Francis Meres, John Davies of Hereford, Ben Jonson, and many others. Indeed, if we make due allowance for the bloating of modern, run-of-the-mill bureaucratic records, more information has survived over the past four hundred years about William Shakespeare of Stratford-upon-Avon, Warwickshire, than is likely to survive in the next four hundred years about any reader of these words.

What we do not have are entire categories of information – Shakespeare's private letters or diaries, drafts and revisions of poems and plays, critical prefaces or essays, commendatory verse for other writers' works, or instructions guiding his fellow actors in their performances, for instance – that we imagine would help us understand and appreciate his surviving writings. For all we know, many such data never existed as written records. Many literary and theatrical critics, not knowing what might once have existed, more or less cheerfully accept the situation; some even make a theoretical virtue of it by claiming that such data are irrelevant to understanding and interpreting the plays and poems.

So, what do we know about William Shakespeare, the man responsible for thirty-seven or perhaps more plays, more than 150 sonnets, two lengthy narrative poems, and some shorter poems?

While many families by the name of Shakespeare (or some variant spelling) can be identified in the English Midlands as far back as the twelfth century, it seems likely that the dramatist's grandfather, Richard, moved to Snitterfield, a town not far from Stratford-upon-Avon, sometime before 1529. In Snitterfield, Richard Shakespeare leased farmland from the very wealthy Robert Arden. By 1552, Richard's son John had moved to a large house on Henley Street in Stratford-upon-Avon, the house that stands today as "The Birthplace." In Stratford, John Shakespeare traded as a glover, dealt in wool, and lent money at interest; he also served in a variety of civic posts, including "High Bailiff," the municipality's equivalent of mayor. In 1557, he married Robert Arden's youngest daughter, Mary. Mary and John had four sons – William was the oldest – and four daughters, of whom only Joan outlived her most celebrated sibling. William was baptized (an event entered in the Stratford parish church records) on April 26, 1564, and it has become customary, without any good factual support, to suppose he was born on April 23, which happens to be the feast day of Saint George, patron saint of England, and is also the date on which he died, in 1616. Shakespeare married Anne Hathaway in 1582, when he was eighteen and she was twenty-six; their first child was born five months later. It has been generally assumed that the marriage was enforced and subsequently unhappy, but these are only assumptions; it has been estimated, for instance, that up to one third of Elizabethan brides were pregnant when they married. Anne and William Shakespeare had three children: Susanna, who married a prominent local physician, John Hall; and the twins Hamnet, who died young in 1596, and Judith, who married Thomas Quiney – apparently a rather shady individual. The name Hamnet was unusual but not unique: he and his twin sister were named for their godparents, Shakespeare's neighbors Hamnet and Judith Sadler. Shakespeare's father died in 1601 (the year of *Hamlet*), and Mary Arden Shakespeare died in 1608 (the year of *Coriolanus*). William Shakespeare's last surviving direct descendant was his granddaughter Elizabeth Hall, who died in 1670.

Between the birth of the twins in 1585 and a clear reference to Shakespeare as a practicing London dramatist in Robert Greene's sensationalizing, satiric pamphlet, *Greene's Groatsworth of Wit* (1592), there is no record of where William Shakespeare was or what he was doing. These seven so-called lost years have been imaginatively filled by scholars and other students of Shakespeare: some think he traveled to Italy, or fought in the Low Countries, or studied law or medicine, or worked as an apprentice actor/writer, and so on to even more fanciful possibilities. Whatever the biographical facts for those "lost" years, Greene's nasty remarks in 1592 testify to professional envy and to the fact that Shakespeare already had a successful career in London. Speaking to his fellow playwrights, Greene warns both generally and specifically:

> . . . trust them [actors] not: for there is an upstart crow, beautified with our feathers, that with his tiger's heart wrapped in a player's hide supposes he is as well able to bombast out a blank verse as the best of you; and being an absolute Johannes Factotum, is in his own conceit the only Shake-scene in a country.

The passage mimics a line from *3 Henry VI* (hence the play must have been performed before Greene wrote) and seems to say that "Shake-scene" is both actor and play-wright, a jack-of-all-trades. That same year, Henry Chettle protested Greene's remarks in *Kind-Heart's Dream*, and each of the next two years saw the publication of poems – *Venus and Adonis* and *The Rape of Lucrece*, respectively – publicly ascribed to (and dedicated by) Shakespeare. Early in 1595 he was named one of the senior members of a prominent acting company, the Lord Chamberlain's Men, when they received payment for court performances during the 1594 Christmas season.

Clearly, Shakespeare had achieved both success and reputation in London. In 1596, upon Shakespeare's application, the College of Arms granted his father the now-familiar coat of arms he had taken the first steps to obtain almost twenty years before, and in 1598, John's son – now permitted to call himself "gentleman" – took a 10 percent share in the new Globe playhouse. In 1597, he bought a substantial bourgeois house, called New Place, in Stratford – the garden remains, but Shakespeare's house, several times rebuilt, was torn down in 1759 – and over the next few years Shakespeare spent large sums buying land and making other investments in the town and its environs. Though he worked in London, his family remained in Stratford, and he seems always to have considered Stratford the home he would eventually return to. Something approaching a disinterested appreciation of Shakespeare's popular and professional status appears in Francis Meres's *Palladis Tamia* (1598), a not especially imaginative and perhaps therefore persuasive record of literary reputations. Reviewing contemporary English writers, Meres lists the titles of many of Shakespeare's plays, including one not now known, *Love's Labor's Won*, and praises his "mellifluous & hony-tongued" "sugred Sonnets," which were then circulating in manuscript (they were first collected in 1609). Meres describes Shakespeare as "one of the best" English playwrights of both comedy and tragedy. In *Remains . . . Concerning Britain* (1605),

William Camden—a more authoritative source than the imitative Meres—calls Shakespeare one of the "most pregnant witts of these our times" and joins him with such writers as Chapman, Daniel, Jonson, Marston, and Spenser. During the first decades of the seventeenth century, publishers began to attribute numerous play quartos, including some non-Shakespearean ones, to Shakespeare, either by name or initials, and we may assume that they deemed Shakespeare's name and supposed authorship, true or false, commercially attractive.

For the next ten years or so, various records show Shakespeare's dual career as playwright and man of the theater in London, and as an important local figure in Stratford. In 1608–9 his acting company—designated the "King's Men" soon after King James had succeeded Queen Elizabeth in 1603—rented, refurbished, and opened a small interior playing space, the Blackfriars theater, in London, and Shakespeare was once again listed as a substantial sharer in the group of proprietors of the playhouse. By May 11, 1612, however, he describes himself as a Stratford resident in a London lawsuit—an indication that he had withdrawn from day-to-day professional activity and returned to the town where he had always had his main financial interests. When Shakespeare bought a substantial residential building in London, the Blackfriars Gatehouse, close to the theater of the same name, on March 10, 1613, he is recorded as William Shakespeare "of Stratford upon Avon in the county of Warwick, gentleman," and he named several London residents as the building's trustees. Still, he continued to participate in theatrical activity: when the new Earl of Rutland needed an allegorical design to bear as a shield, or *impresa,* at the celebration of King James's Accession Day, March 24, 1613, the earl's accountant recorded a payment of 44 shillings to Shakespeare for the device with its motto.

For the last few years of his life, Shakespeare evidently

concentrated his activities in the town of his birth. Most of the final records concern business transactions in Stratford, ending with the notation of his death on April 23, 1616, and burial in Holy Trinity Church, Stratford-upon-Avon.

THE QUESTION OF AUTHORSHIP

The history of ascribing Shakespeare's plays (the poems do not come up so often) to someone else began, as it continues, peculiarly. The earliest published claim that someone else wrote Shakespeare's plays appeared in an 1856 article by Delia Bacon in the American journal *Putnam's Monthly* – although an Englishman, Thomas Wilmot, had shared his doubts in private (even secretive) conversations with friends near the end of the eighteenth century. Bacon's was a sad personal history that ended in madness and poverty, but the year after her article, she published, with great difficulty and the bemused assistance of Nathaniel Hawthorne (then United States Consul in Liverpool, England), her *Philosophy of the Plays of Shakspere Unfolded.* This huge, ornately written, confusing farrago is almost unreadable; sometimes its intents, to say nothing of its arguments, disappear entirely beneath near-raving, ecstatic writing. Tumbled in with much supposed "philosophy" appear the claims that Francis Bacon (from whom Delia Bacon eventually claimed descent), Walter Ralegh, and several other contemporaries of Shakespeare's had written the plays. The book had little impact except as a ridiculed curiosity.

Once proposed, however, the issue gained momentum among people whose conviction was the greater in proportion to their ignorance of sixteenth- and seventeenth-century English literature, history, and society. Another American amateur, Catherine P. Ashmead Windle, made the next influential contribution to the cause when she published *Report to the British Museum* (1882), wherein she promised to open "the Cipher of Francis Bacon," though what she mostly offers, in the words of S. Schoenbaum, is "demented allegorizing." An entire new cottage industry grew from Windle's suggestion that the texts contain hidden, cryptographically discoverable ciphers – "clues" – to their authorship; and today there are not only books devoted to the putative ciphers, but also pamphlets, journals, and newsletters.

Although Baconians have led the pack of those seeking a substitute Shakespeare, in *"Shakespeare" Identified* (1920), J. Thomas Looney became the first published "Oxfordian" when he proposed Edward de Vere, seventeenth earl of Oxford, as the secret author of Shakespeare's plays. Also for Oxford and his "authorship" there are today dedicated societies, articles, journals, and books. Less popular candidates – Queen Elizabeth and Christopher Marlowe among them – have had adherents, but the movement seems to have divided into two main contending factions, Baconian and Oxfordian. (For further details on all the candidates for "Shakespeare," see S. Schoenbaum, *Shakespeare's Lives*, 2nd ed., 1991.)

The Baconians, the Oxfordians, and supporters of other candidates have one trait in common – they are snobs. Every pro-Bacon or pro-Oxford tract sooner or later claims that the historical William Shakespeare of Stratford-upon-Avon could not have written the plays because he could not have had the training, the university education, the experience, and indeed the imagination or background their author supposedly possessed. Only a learned genius like Bacon or an aristocrat like Oxford could have written such fine plays. (As it happens, lucky male children of the middle class had access to better education than most aristocrats in Elizabethan England – and Oxford was not particularly well educated.) Shakespeare received in the Stratford grammar school a formal education that would daunt many college graduates today; and popular rival playwrights such as the very learned Ben Jonson and George Chapman, both of whom also lacked university training, achieved great artistic success, without being taken as Bacon or Oxford.

Besides snobbery, one other quality characterizes the authorship controversy: lack of evidence. A great deal of testimony from Shakespeare's time shows that Shakespeare wrote Shakespeare's plays and that his contemporaries recognized them as distinctive and distinctly superior. (Some of that contemporary evidence is collected in E. K. Chambers, *William Shakespeare: A Study of Facts and Problems,* 2 vols., 1930.) Since that testimony comes from Shakespeare's enemies and theatrical competitors as well as from his co-workers and from the Elizabethan equivalent of literary journalists, it seems unlikely that, if any one of these sources had known he was a fraud, they would have failed to record that fact.

Books About Shakespeare's Theater

Useful scholarly studies of theatrical life in Shakespeare's day include: G. E. Bentley, *The Jacobean and Caroline Stage,* 7 vols. (1941-68), and the same author's *The Professions of Dramatist and Player in Shakespeare's Time, 1590-1642* (1986); E. K. Chambers, *The Elizabethan Stage,* 4 vols. (1923); R. A. Foakes, *Illustrations of the English Stage, 1580-1642* (1985); Andrew Gurr, *The Shakespearean Stage,* 3rd ed. (1992), and the same author's *Play-going in Shakespeare's London,* 2nd ed. (1996); Edwin Nungezer, *A Dictionary of Actors* (1929); Carol Chillington Rutter, ed., *Documents of the Rose Playhouse* (1984).

Books About Shakespeare's Life

The following books provide scholarly, documented accounts of Shakespeare's life: G. E. Bentley, *Shakespeare: A Biographical Handbook* (1961); E. K. Chambers, *William Shakespeare: A Study of Facts and Problems,* 2 vols. (1930); S. Schoenbaum, *William Shakespeare: A Compact*

Documentary Life (1977); and *Shakespeare's Lives,* 2nd ed. (1991), by the same author. Many scholarly editions of Shakespeare's complete works print brief compilations of essential dates and events. References to Shakespeare's works up to 1700 are collected in C. M. Ingleby et al., *The Shakespeare Allusion-Book,* rev. ed., 2 vols. (1932).

The Texts of Shakespeare

As far as we know, only one manuscript conceivably in Shakespeare's own hand may (and even this is much disputed) exist: a few pages of a play called *Sir Thomas More*, which apparently was never performed. What we do have, as later readers, performers, scholars, students, are printed texts. The earliest of these survive in two forms: quartos and folios. Quartos (from the Latin for "four") are small books, printed on sheets of paper that were then folded in fours, to make eight double-sided pages. When these were bound together, the result was a squarish, eminently portable volume that sold for the relatively small sum of sixpence (translating in modern terms to about $5.00). In folios, on the other hand, the sheets are folded only once, in half, producing large, impressive volumes taller than they are wide. This was the format for important works of philosophy, science, theology, and literature (the major precedent for a folio Shakespeare was Ben Jonson's *Works*, 1616). The decision to print the works of a popular playwright in folio is an indication of how far up on the social scale the theatrical profession had come during Shakespeare's lifetime. The Shakespeare folio was an expensive book, selling for between fifteen and eighteen shillings, depending on the binding (in modern terms, from about $150 to $180). Twenty Shakespeare plays of the thirty-seven that survive first appeared in quarto, seventeen of which appeared during Shakespeare's lifetime; the rest of the plays are found only in folio.

The First Folio was published in 1623, seven years after Shakespeare's death, and was authorized by his fellow actors, the co-owners of the King's Men. This publication was certainly a mark of the company's enormous respect for Shakespeare; but it was also a way of turning the old plays, most of which were no longer current in the playhouse, into ready money (the folio includes only Shakespeare's plays, not his sonnets or other nondramatic verse). Whatever the motives behind the publication of the folio, the texts it preserves constitute the basis for almost all later editions of the playwright's works. The texts, however, differ from those of the earlier quartos, sometimes in minor respects but often significantly – most strikingly in the two texts of *King Lear*, but also in important ways in *Hamlet, Othello,* and *Troilus and Cressida.* (The variants are recorded in the textual notes to each play in the new Pelican series.) The differences in these texts represent, in a sense, the essence of theater: the texts of plays were initially not intended for publication. They were scripts, designed for the actors to perform – the principal life of the play at this period was in performance. And it follows that in Shakespeare's theater the playwright typically had no say either in how his play was performed or in the disposition of his text – he was an employee of the company. The authoritative figures in the theatrical enterprise were the shareholders in the company, who were for the most part the major actors. They decided what plays were to be done; they hired the playwright and often gave him an outline of the play they wanted him to write. Often, too, the play was a collaboration: the company would retain a group of writers, and parcel out the scenes among them. The resulting script was then the property of the company, and the actors would revise it as they saw fit during the course of putting it on stage. The resulting text belonged to the company. The playwright had no rights in it once he had been paid. (This system survives largely intact in the movie industry, and most of the playwrights of Shakespeare's time were as anonymous as most screenwriters are today.) The script could also, of course, continue to change as the tastes of audiences and the requirements of the actors changed. Many – perhaps most – plays were revised when they were reintroduced after any substantial absence from the repertory, or when they were performed by a company different from the one that originally commissioned the play.

Shakespeare was an exceptional figure in this world because he was not only a shareholder and actor in his company, but also its leading playwright – he was literally his own boss. He had, moreover, little interest in the publication of his plays, and even those that appeared during his lifetime with the authorization of the company show no signs of any editorial concern on the part of the author. Theater was, for Shakespeare, a fluid and supremely responsive medium – the very opposite of the great classic canonical text that has embodied his works since 1623.

The very fluidity of the original texts, however, has meant that Shakespeare has always had to be edited. Here is an example of how problematic the editorial project inevitably is, a passage from the most famous speech in *Romeo and Juliet*, Juliet's balcony soliloquy beginning "O Romeo, Romeo, wherefore art thou Romeo?" Since the eighteenth century, the standard modern text has read,

> What's Montague? It is nor hand, nor foot,
> Nor arm, nor face, nor any other part
> Belonging to a man. O be some other name!
> What's in a name? That which we call a rose
> By any other name would smell as sweet.
>
> (II.2.40–44)

Editors have three early texts of this play to work from, two quarto texts and the folio. Here is how the First Quarto (1597) reads:

> Whats *Mountague?* It is nor band nor foote,
> Nor arme, nor face, nor any other part.
> Whats in a name? That which we call a Rofe,
> By any other name would fmell as fweet:

Here is the Second Quarto (1599):

> Whats *Mountague?* it is nor hand nor foote,
> Nor arme nor face, ô be fome other name
> Belonging to a man.
> Whats in a name that which we call a rofe,
> By any other word would fmell as fweete,

And here is the First Folio (1623):

> What's *Mountague?* it is nor hand nor foote,
> Nor arme, nor face, O be fome other name
> Belonging to a man.
> What? in a names that which we call a Rofe,
> By any other word would fmell as fweete,

There is in fact no early text that reads as our modern text does – and this is the most famous speech in the play. Instead, we have three quite different texts, all of which are clearly some version of the same speech, but none of which seems to us a final or satisfactory version. The transcendently beautiful passage in modern editions is an editorial invention: editors have succeeded in conflating and revising the three versions into something we recognize as great poetry. Is this what Shakespeare "really" wrote? Who can say? What we can say is that Shakespeare always had performance, not a book, in mind.

Books About the Shakespeare Texts

The standard study of the printing history of the First Folio is W. W. Greg, *The Shakespeare First Folio* (1955). J. K. Walton, *The Quarto Copy for the First Folio of Shakespeare* (1971), is a useful survey of the relation of the quartos to the folio. The second edition of Charlton Hinman's *Norton Facsimile* of the First Folio (1996), with a new introduction by Peter Blayney, is indispensable. Stanley Wells and Gary Taylor, *William Shakespeare: A Textual Companion*, keyed to the Oxford text, gives a comprehensive survey of the editorial situation for all the plays and poems.

THE GENERAL EDITORS

Introduction

THE COMEDY OF ERRORS was long considered an apprentice piece written before Shakespeare reached the height of his powers – derivative, slapstick, slight. Onstage, it is often played as more visual than verbal, a mayhem of mugging and whacking. It would be difficult to view the play as anything other than rowdy: its plot depends on one running joke of mistaken identity, which leads to various kinds of confusion and abuse. Increasingly, however, critics have been seeing this rowdiness as inseparable from the more serious concerns that motivate and complicate it. To point to the grief, slavery, violence, anger, and threatened execution in the play is not to point away from the comedy in it, but rather to probe its center. The play robustly explores the anxieties that emerge from suffering, deprivation, and uncertainty.

The Comedy of Errors thus provides a case study in the fine, unstable line between comedy and tragedy. Egeon, for instance, thinks he is in a tragedy, and for years he has been; he has longed for the miserable death that would bring his tragedy to closure – the death with which he is threatened until the very end of the play. The genre of his life is transformed, as is so much else in this play, by a shift in perspective. The spotlight broadens from the suffering individual of tragedy to the larger and hardier communities of comedy, from the inevitability of death to the possibility of reconciliation, renewal, and rebirth. The audience is in the unique position of occupying both points of view, the tragic and the comic, since we know what no one onstage does: that both sets of twins are in Ephesus. The play is sharply focused, with the action occurring in one place on a single day, yet preoccupied with fragmentation and multiplicity. Its actions can be considered not only as comedy or tragedy, but also as farce, horror, and romance. In this mixture of tones and forms, *The Comedy of Errors* does not stand apart from Shakespeare's other plays but bears close connections both to his last plays (often called the romances) and to his earliest.

   The Comedy of Errors is assumed to be an early play, but we know for sure only that the first recorded performance was given at the Gray's Inn Christmas Revels, December 28, 1594. This means that the audience would have been lawyers and law students (largely men, with some women present by invitation). Shakespeare may have written the play just before this performance or, as some think, years earlier. Scholars have attempted to fix the date by reference to other plays or to contemporary events, such as the French Civil War (c. 1589-93). Since none of the referents are themselves fixed – the dates of the French Civil War, for instance, might reasonably be extended both earlier and later – these topical references cannot prove much about the dates of the play's composition or performance. It was first printed in the First Folio (1623).

   However early *The Comedy of Errors* came in Shakespeare's career, in it he exhibits what became a characteristic relation to sources (that is, earlier versions of similar stories) – borrowing freely, but also creatively, adapting and transforming. The earlier work that most closely resembles *The Comedy of Errors* is the Roman comedy *Menaechmi,* by Plautus (c. 254-184 B.C.). Shakespeare's Latin may have been good enough to enable him to read Plautus's play in the original Latin, or he may have relied on a translation by W. W., which, while not entered in the Stationers' Register until 1594, may have circulated in manuscript considerably earlier. Again, it is impossible to be sure. In adapting *Menaechmi,* Shakespeare made many changes, including doubling the twins, by adding twin slaves for the twin masters; expanding the role of the wife and demoting the Courtesan to a minor player; introducing the wife's sister, Luciana, a love interest for the Syracusan twin; combining two characters, the Courtesan's maid and cook, into one, Luce/Nell (whose two names suggest that Shakespeare may have revised the play to eliminate the confusion caused by the similarity between the names Luciana and Luce); and adding the Egeon-Emilia framework.

Shakespeare also seems to have borrowed the lock-out scene (III.1), in which Adriana, thinking Antipholus of Syracuse is her husband, entertains him. In Plautus's *Amphitruo*, a master is kept out while the god Jupiter, impersonating him, is entertained. Since the Plautus version makes it clear that the entertainment is sexual, many have also surmised that Adriana offers Antipholus of Syracuse more than dinner. Other texts to which *The Comedy of Errors* bears some resemblance, or owes some debt, include George Gascoigne's *Supposes*, a prose version of Ariosto's *I Suppositi* printed in 1575, which also seems to have influenced *The Taming of the Shrew*; and John Gower's *Apollonius of Tyre*, which was also an influence on *Pericles* (a play that bears various similarities to *The Comedy of Errors*, especially in its ending). More generally, *The Comedy of Errors* seems to have been informed by Italian comedy, by the plays of Shakespeare's contemporaries such as Lyly, by the native English comic tradition that focuses on the abusive or shrewish wife, and even by early humanist ideas about marriage, such as those of Erasmus.

To list Shakespeare's sources and influences is not to suggest that we can reconstruct what Shakespeare read or knew, or that, if we could, this would explain why he wrote a particular play or why it took the form it did. Nor does it necessarily suggest a simple linear progression from the origin or "source" to the end product, the revision or adaptation that stands as the last word. A consideration of other available versions of a given plot, for instance, presents Shakespeare as a writer who cleverly exploited available cultural materials rather than conceiving utterly new situations, characters, and plots. If Shakespeare's claim to fame does not lie in inventing new stories, then perhaps it lies in his ability to identify the issues and stories of greatest appeal to a broad audience, and to create, in large part through judicious borrowing and creative recombination, especially compelling versions of popular stories. Why does Shakespeare choose to retell a Plautine story? To what end does he make the changes that he does? How does he give the familiar story new purchase in his own cultural moment? Such questions consider Shakespeare as an active participant in his own times. For the most part, Shakespeare shares with other writers a similar bag of concerns, conventions, and forms; he thus articulates views we can find elsewhere in his culture, as he shapes how people look at and talk about the issues that interest them.

To consider Shakespeare's play as one possible version among many is quite in the spirit of the play's setting — the magical, perhaps a bit threatening, world of Ephesus. Ephesus is a "fairyland" in which people are "transformèd" (II.2.188, 194). As Antipholus of Syracuse reflects,

> They say this town is full of cozenage:
> As, nimble jugglers that deceive the eye,
> Dark-working sorcerers that change the mind,
> Soul-killing witches that deform the body,
> Disguisèd cheaters, prating mountebanks,
> And many suchlike liberties of sin
>
> (I.2.97–102)

As this description makes clear, such magic is not necessarily benign. Elizabethan statutes making witchcraft a crime suggest that many people took "dark-working sorcerers" and "soul-killing witches" very seriously indeed, attributing to them the power to destroy property and health, to invade and undermine the home and the body, to steal sanity, identity, and life. Later, as the seventeenth century unfolded, the urban elite came to view occult practices with increasing skepticism and, therefore, with increasing mirth rather than fear. For such people, sorcerers and mountebanks, magic and trickery became indistinguishable.

But *The Comedy of Errors* precedes this chic irreverence; performed in the 1590s, when prosecutions in England were at their height, the play finds humor not in magic but in characters who misinterpret the cause of their confusion. As the audience knows, Antipholus of Syracuse is being confused and deceived not through magic or trickery but by the extraordinary circumstance of stumbling into his twin's life. Yet the darker possibilities of witchcraft lurk beneath the comedy; from the point of view of the two sets of twins, identity itself seems to be at risk:

> Am I in earth, in heaven, or in hell?
> Sleeping or waking? mad or well advised?
> Known unto these, and to myself disguised!
> (II.2.211–13)

Ephesus seems, in some ways, outside time and place; the play also conjoins disparate historical moments and systems of belief. In it, Elizabethan debt officers and Roman slaves coexist. So, too, do references to pre-Christian and Christian cultures: Plautus's plays describe a pre-Christian world, yet Ephesus also has New Testament resonances, from Paul's epistle to the Ephesians and Acts 19. Many of the references to faith in the play are not to the pre-Christian or early Christian beliefs of Plautus or Paul, nor to the dominant faith in Shakespeare's England, but to the faith of England's recent past – that is, Roman Catholicism. This "fairyland," like the never-never land in many Elizabethan and later romances, seems largely untouched by the Reformation. When Dromio cries "O, for my beads! I cross me for a sinner. / This is the fairyland" (II.2.187–88), his reference to rosary beads and to crossing himself marks him as distinctly (and comi-cally) Catholic. Possession of rosary beads became, under Elizabeth, criminal; crossing oneself was a risky public performance of Catholic faith. There are also references in the play to shriving (or the sacrament of confession), exorcism (IV.4.55-58), and taking sanctuary. These references to Catholic beliefs and practices help to demonstrate the foolishness of the characters, as well as the inefficacy of their beliefs.

Yet, in the abbess, the play presents a lost possibility with some reverence. The abbess has had an option that the Reformation in England foreclosed for women – en-tering a convent. Although nuns were often stock comic figures, here the abbess is dignified and authoritative. She is, as has often been remarked, a character from the plays of Shakespeare's final years, which depict similarly magi-cal worlds. One consequence of that magic is that what was lost can be found, and that mothers, safely removed from the action as their children mature, can be restored to an iconic, if not an active, role in the family. Drawing on traditions of the representation of goddesses and priestesses in antiquity, and female saints and the Virgin Mary in Catholicism, the role of the abbess marks a fan-tasy return not just of the lost mother, presumed dead, but of the powerful female religious figure for which Protestantism, much more focused on the Father and the Son, could not find a space. In its depiction of her, *The Comedy of Errors* hints at the possibility that Catholicism is not a childish religion of the past, suited only to a bum-bling servant, but can be associated with a lost, lamented, and longed-for mother, who, on her reappearance, might resolve everything.

While Dromio of Syracuse reaches for his rosary beads, his master copes with this uncertain and unstable world by surrendering to it. In many of Shakespeare's comedies, there are those who learn to play along and those who refuse or fail, and are therefore excluded from the festive conclusion. Antipholus of Syracuse decides, "I'll entertain the offered fallacy" (II.2.185) and "I'll say as they say, and persever so, / And in this mist at all adventures go" (II.2.214-15). To a certain extent, it is easier for him to say this than for Antipholus of Ephesus – since he gains in the confusion (a wife, a gold chain, an object of desire), while his brother loses. Still, the choice to submit to rather than indignantly resist counterfeits, games, and illusions usually distinguishes the survivors and winners from the losers in Shakespeare's comic worlds. As Antipholus of Syracuse says to Luciana, "Transform me then, and to your power I'll yield" (III.2.40). Such submissiveness, from which this Antipholus reaps such great rewards, corresponds to patience, that crucial marital virtue to which the play's various marriage counselors frequently refer.

How are the play's homilies on matrimony connected to its central plot about mistaken identity? While many of Shakespeare's plays explore the difficulty of understanding and accommodating difference (whether of gender, race, nationality, class, or sexuality), *The Comedy of Errors* explores the difficulties of comprehending similarity. Certainly, there are gender conflicts between husband and wife, and class conflicts between masters and servants. Yet most of the action focuses on the mystery and mayhem of sameness, of two people with one identity. Marriage might be considered to pose the same dilemma as identical twins: How can two become one, "undividable, incorporate" (II.2.121)?

That the play includes so much marital advice suggests that union does not come easily. It is also telling that female characters living outside marriage deliver the advice. Unmarried Luciana lectures her sister, Adriana, on men's natural superiority and sway, and on women's subservience (II.1), in a lengthy speech that bears a striking resemblance to Kate's lecture to other wives at the end of *The Taming of the Shrew.* Luciana also lectures the man she takes to be her brother-in-law, on masking infidelity by dissembling (III.2). Finally, the long-celibate abbess lectures Adriana, blaming her for driving her husband crazy by nagging him (V.1). All of these lessons offer the most conventional marital advice available at the time, by assigning wives an unambiguously subordinate role and advising them to bite their tongues and suppress their feelings. More complex views of the wife's role and of women's possibilities were in circulation in sixteenth-century England. These lectures, then, may operate as the references to Catholicism do; they may suggest that the play's world is dated, its characters' values obsolete and inadequate. Adhering to outmoded, rigid, even ineffectual solutions, the characters exacerbate rather than resolve their dilemmas. For, no matter how patient Adriana might be, she would still have two increasingly bewildered – and in the case of Antipholus of Ephesus, irate – husbands, until they confront each other. Would it be morally preferable for her to submit to two men, whom, disturbingly, she cannot tell apart, offering "entertainment" to both? The plot pulls against the marital advice: conflict is resolved not by submerging oneself but by clearly distinguishing between one and another, not by blurring distinctions but by clarifying them.

That the play's first reference to Adriana is Dromio of Ephesus's remark on her violence (I.2.46) works to locate her in the shrew tradition, which depicts unruly women as both physically and verbally abusive. The abbess's lengthy censure of Adriana also locates her in this tradition, in which a wife makes the bed and board, which should be respites for her husband, locations of discomfort. In the most conventional terms, we are told that one of the principal causes of disorder in this world is women, particularly the wife who is jealous, nagging, and abusive. Yet this is very much at odds with the plot. The abbess is wrong about the cause of Antipholus's madness. The cause of disorder in Ephesus is the multiplying of men, not the nagging of women. It is not insubordinate wives and servants who threaten the authority (and sanity) of husbands and masters, but their own doubles, who reveal that they are not unique and can be replaced.

How alike are the two Antipholuses? While they are visually indistinguishable, critics have attempted to differentiate their characters in various ways. One approach is to compare their levels of violence and their relationships with their slaves. In a tally of blows, Antipholus of Ephesus comes out ahead. Antipholus of Syracuse may strike the first blow we see in the play (according to the text, anyway), but it is his brother's slave, Dromio of Ephesus, who seems to have a long history of beatings. Dromio complains of having had "nothing at his [master's] hands for my service but blows" and anticipates being so lamed by brutality that he will have to beg for his living (IV.4.30–39). Yet, while this suggests that Antipholus of Ephesus has routinely beaten his servant, Adriana takes the one beating she witnesses as proof of her husband's madness (IV.4) rather than as commonplace.

The play depicts violence as the province of those with power, who inflict it both to express anger and to discipline. Like slave owners, the state, as represented by the Duke of Ephesus, also employs violence to enforce law and maintain order; the threat of execution hangs over the play, reminding us that violence can sometimes have fatal consequences. For the most part, however, those consequences are forgotten, in slapstick depictions of distracted and disorderly violence that do much of the work of showing two men maddened by confusion and increasingly out of control.

To say that the violence is presented comically is not to discount it, but to question it and the reactions it invites. This violence draws on a long-standing tradition of presenting violence as comic, a tradition that reaches back to Plautine comedy, in which masters constantly threaten to beat, mutilate, and crucify their servants/slaves; the tradition also includes early English stories and jokes. This tradition generally presents violence from the perspective of the aggravated authority figure who inflicts the cruelty, rather than from the perspective of the subordinate who suffers it.

Yet, in *The Comedy of Errors* Dromio of Ephesus constantly brings his experience, and the lingering consequences of violence, to his master's, and the audience's, attention. For instance, he presents his body as a record of the beatings he has received, complaining to Antipholus of Ephesus, who denies having beaten him: "That you beat me at the mart, I have your hand to show. / If the skin were parchment and the blows you gave were ink, / Your own handwriting would tell you what I think" (III.1.12-14). According to Egeon, emotional suffering, too, writes on faces: "Time's deformèd hand, / Ha[s] written strange defeatures in my face" (V.1.299-300). One of the ways productions of this play might keep the violence within the confines of farce – that is, divorced from suffering and consequence – is by leaving both Dromios unmarked. If they became progressively bruised or were limping, the humor in injury would become even more strained than it is.

Violence is also rendered farcical when its targets are depicted as not-quite-human, another strategy for repressing the experience of being beaten. To a certain extent slavery, in Plautine drama and in *The Comedy of Errors*, suggests that the characters who are most often beaten and threatened make different – lesser – claims on our sympathies. Again, however, the vociferous Dromios – especially Dromio of Ephesus – upset this convention by insisting on their pain and indignation, by demanding attention. Their objections to abusive treatment both remind us of their suffering, thus making the violence more disturbing, and comment on their status as slaves, suggesting that their claims on our attention, sympathy, and interest are equal to, and perhaps even greater than, their masters'. Considering the violence in the play is thus one way not only of contrasting the Antipholuses, but also of assessing the delicate balance of serious and silly in this deceptively simple play. To press too hard on the points of connection between this play and more sober controversies about domestic relations is to mistake the tone; but to dwell only on the nimble juggling is to miss the serious issues that seek release through laughter and magical transformation.

FRANCES E. DOLAN
Miami University, Ohio

Note on the Text

THE COMEDY OF ERRORS was first printed in the folio of 1623. Except for considerable confusion of character names in the stage directions and speech prefixes, the text is a good one. There is indication (see V.1.9 s.d.) that the folio act division was superimposed upon the original manuscript, but this division, with a further division of the acts into scenes, is provided for reference in the present edition. The following brief list of departures from the folio text is complete, except for the correction of obvious typographical errors and the normalization of speech prefixes and of such forms as the following in the stage directions: *Antipholus Ephes.* (to *Antipholus of Ephesus*), *Antipholus Siracusia* (to *Antipholus of Syracuse*), and *S. Dromio* (to *Dromio of Syracuse*). The adopted reading in italics is followed by the folio reading in roman.

I.1   16 *at* at any   41 (and throughout) *Epidamnum* Epidamium   42 *the* he   102 *upon* up   116 *bark* bank   123 *thee* they   151 *life* help
I.2   s.d. *Antipholus [of Syracuse]* Antipholis Erotes   4 *arrival* a rival   30 *lose* loose   32 s.d. *Exit* Exeunt   40 *unhappy* unhappy a   65 *score* scour   66 *clock* cook   93 *God's* God   94 s.d. *Exit* Exeunt
II.1   s.d. *Antipholus [of Ephesus]* Antipholis Sereptus   11 *o' door* adore   12 *ill* thus   20 *Men* Man;   *masters* master   21 *Lords* Lord   45 *two* too 61 *thousand* hundred   72 *errand* arrant   112 *Wear* Where
II.2   s.d. *Antipholus [of Syracuse]* Antipholis Errotis   12 *didst* did didst   79 *men* them   97 *tiring* trying   101 *no time* in no time   135 *off* of   174 *stronger* stranger   185 *offered* free'd   193 *drone* Dromio
III.1   75 *you* your   89 *her* your   91 *her* your
III.2   s.d. *Luciana* Juliana   4 *building* buildings;   *ruinous* ruinate   16 *attaint* attaine   21 *but* not   26 *wife* wise   46 *sister's* sister   49 *bed* bud;   *them* thee   57 *where* when   109 *and* is
IV.1   17 *her* their   87 *then* then sir
IV.2   6 *Of* Oh   34 *One* On   45 *a's* is   48 *That* Thus   61 *a* I
IV.3   24 *'rests* rests   34 *ship* ships   58 *if you do* if do
IV.4   3 *'rested* rested
V.1   33 *God's* God   121 *death* depth   155 *whither* whether   306 *Ay, sir* I sir   358–63 (in F these lines follow l. 347)   405 *ne'er* are

The Comedy of Errors

[NAMES OF THE ACTORS

SOLINUS, *Duke of Ephesus*
EGEON, *a merchant of Syracuse*
ANTIPHOLUS OF EPHESUS } *twin brothers, and sons*
ANTIPHOLUS OF SYRACUSE } *to Egeon and Emilia, but*
unknown to each other
DROMIO OF EPHESUS } *twin brothers, and slaves to the*
DROMIO OF SYRACUSE } *two Antipholuses*
BALTHASAR, *a merchant*
ANGELO, *a goldsmith*
A MERCHANT, *friend to Antipholus of Syracuse*
A SECOND MERCHANT, *to whom Angelo is a debtor*
DR. PINCH, *a schoolmaster and a conjurer*
EMILIA, *wife to Egeon, an abbess at Ephesus*
ADRIANA, *wife to Antipholus of Ephesus*
LUCIANA, *sister to Adriana*
LUCE, *servant to Adriana*
A COURTESAN
JAILER, OFFICERS, AND OTHER ATTENDANTS

SCENE: *Ephesus*]

The Comedy of Errors

I.1 *Enter the Duke of Ephesus, with the Merchant [Egeon] of Syracuse, Jailer, and other Attendants.*

EGEON

Proceed, Solinus, to procure my fall,
And by the doom of death end woes and all.

DUKE

Merchant of Syracusa, plead no more.
I am not partial to infringe our laws. 4
The enmity and discord which of late
Sprung from the rancorous outrage of your duke
To merchants, our well-dealing countrymen,
Who, wanting guilders to redeem their lives, 8
Have sealed his rigorous statutes with their bloods,
Excludes all pity from our threat'ning looks. 10
For since the mortal and intestine jars 11
'Twixt thy seditious countrymen and us,
It hath in solemn synods been decreed, 13
Both by the Syracusians and ourselves,
To admit no traffic to our adverse towns: 15
Nay more, if any born at Ephesus 16
Be seen at Syracusian marts and fairs;
Again, if any Syracusian born
Come to the bay of Ephesus, he dies,

I.1 In Ephesus, presumably the palace of Duke Solinus **4** *partial* inclined
8 *guilders* (Dutch coins worth about 7p. apiece) **11** *intestine* (usually means
"internal"; here, perhaps, intensifies *mortal*) **13** *synods* councils **15** *adverse*
opposed **16** *Ephesus* (on west coast of Asia Minor)

20   His goods confiscate to the duke's dispose,
21   Unless a thousand marks be levièd,
22   To quit the penalty and to ransom him.
      Thy substance, valued at the highest rate,
      Cannot amount unto a hundred marks;
      Therefore, by law thou art condemned to die.

EGEON
      Yet this my comfort: when your words are done,
      My woes end likewise with the evening sun.

DUKE
      Well, Syracusian, say in brief the cause
      Why thou departed'st from thy native home,
30   And for what cause thou cam'st to Ephesus.

EGEON
      A heavier task could not have been imposed
      Than I to speak my griefs unspeakable;
      Yet that the world may witness that my end
34   Was wrought by nature, not by vile offense,
      I'll utter what my sorrow gives me leave.
      In Syracusa was I born, and wed
      Unto a woman, happy but for me,
38   And by me, had not our hap been bad.
      With her I lived in joy: our wealth increased
40   By prosperous voyages I often made
41   To Epidamnum; till my factor's death,
      And the great care of goods at random left,
      Drew me from kind embracements of my spouse;
      From whom my absence was not six months old,
      Before herself (almost at fainting under
      The pleasing punishment that women bear)
      Had made provision for her following me,
      And soon and safe arrivèd where I was.

---

21 *marks* (worth about 13s. 4d. apiece)   22 *quit* discharge, pay   34 *nature*
natural – i.e., fatherly – love   38 *hap* luck   41 *Epidamnum* i.e., Epidamnus,
port on the east coast of the Adriatic ("Epidamnum" was the form used by
W W [William Warner?] in his translation of the Latin source, 1595);
factor's agent's

There had she not been long but she became
A joyful mother of two goodly sons;   50
And, which was strange, the one so like the other
As could not be distinguished but by names.
That very hour, and in the self-same inn,
A mean woman was deliverèd   54
Of such a burden male, twins both alike.
Those – for their parents were exceeding poor –
I bought, and brought up to attend my sons.
My wife, not meanly proud of two such boys,   58
Made daily motions for our home return.   59
Unwilling I agreed. Alas! too soon   60
We came aboard.
A league from Epidamnum had we sailed
Before the always wind-obeying deep
Gave any tragic instance of our harm.   64
But longer did we not retain much hope;
For what obscurèd light the heavens did grant
Did but convey unto our fearful minds
A doubtful warrant of immediate death;   68
Which, though myself would gladly have embraced,
Yet the incessant weepings of my wife,   70
Weeping before for what she saw must come,
And piteous plainings of the pretty babes,   72
That mourned for fashion, ignorant what to fear,   73
Forced me to seek delays for them and me.
And this it was, for other means was none:
The sailors sought for safety by our boat,
And left the ship, then sinking-ripe, to us.   77
My wife, more careful for the latter-born,   78
Had fastened him unto a small spare mast,
Such as seafaring men provide for storms;   80

---

54 *mean* of low birth   58 *not meanly* more than commonly   59 *motions* plea
64 *instance* clear indication   68 *doubtful warrant* disturbing omen
72 *plainings* crying   73 *for fashion* (because their mother and brothers did)
77 *sinking-ripe* ready to sink   78 *My . . . latter-born* (l. 124 indicates, puzzlingly, that not the "latter-born," but the elder, went with the mother)

To him one of the other twins was bound,
Whilst I had been like heedful of the other.
The children thus disposed, my wife and I,
Fixing our eyes on whom our care was fixed,
Fastened ourselves at either end the mast,
And floating straight, obedient to the stream,
Was carried towards Corinth, as we thought.
At length the sun, gazing upon the earth,
Dispersed those vapors that offended us,

90 And by the benefit of his wishèd light
The seas waxed calm, and we discoverèd

92 Two ships from far, making amain to us:

93 Of Corinth that, of Epidaurus this.
But ere they came – O let me say no more!
Gather the sequel by that went before.

DUKE
Nay, forward, old man; do not break off so,
For we may pity, though not pardon thee.

EGEON
O, had the gods done so, I had not now
Worthily termed them merciless to us!

100 For ere the ships could meet by twice five leagues,
We were encountered by a mighty rock,
Which being violently borne upon,

103 Our helpful ship was splitted in the midst;
So that, in this unjust divorce of us,
Fortune had left to both of us alike,
What to delight in, what to sorrow for.
Her part, poor soul, seeming as burdenèd
With lesser weight, but not with lesser woe,
Was carried with more speed before the wind,

110 And in our sight they three were taken up
By fishermen of Corinth, as we thought.
At length another ship had seized on us,

---

92 *amain* speed **93** *Epidaurus* (town in Argolis on the Saronic Gulf) **103** *helpful ship* i.e., the mast

And knowing whom it was their hap to save,
Gave healthful welcome to their ship-wracked guests,
And would have reft the fishers of their prey,   115
Had not their bark been very slow of sail;   116
And therefore homeward did they bend their course.
Thus have you heard me severed from my bliss,
That by misfortunes was my life prolonged,
To tell sad stories of my own mishaps.   120

DUKE
And for the sake of them thou sorrowest for,
Do me the favor to dilate at full,   122
What have befall'n of them and thee till now.

EGEON
My youngest boy, and yet my eldest care,
At eighteen years became inquisitive
After his brother; and importuned me
That his attendant – so his case was like,   127
Reft of his brother, but retained his name –
Might bear him company in the quest of him;
Whom whilst I labored of a love to see,   130
I hazarded the loss of whom I loved.
Five summers have I spent in farthest Greece,
Roaming clean through the bounds of Asia,
And coasting homeward, came to Ephesus,
Hopeless to find, yet loath to leave unsought
Or that or any place that harbors men.   136
But here must end the story of my life;
And happy were I in my timely death,   138
Could all my travels warrant me they live.   139

DUKE
Hapless Egeon, whom the fates have marked   140
To bear the extremity of dire mishap!

---

115 *reft* robbed 116 *bark* small ship 122 *dilate* describe at length, expand
on 127–28 *attendant . . . name* (referring to the slaves, each named
Dromio) 130 *of a love* out of love 136 *Or . . . or* either . . . or 138 *timely*
speedy 139 *travels* (with a secondary sense of "travails" or labors)

Now trust me, were it not against our laws,
Against my crown, my oath, my dignity,
144   Which princes, would they, may not disannul,
My soul should sue as advocate for thee.
146   But though thou art adjudgèd to the death,
And passèd sentence may not be recalled
But to our honor's great disparagement,
Yet will I favor thee in what I can.
150   Therefore, merchant, I'll limit thee this day
151   To seek thy life by beneficial help.
Try all the friends thou hast in Ephesus;
Beg thou, or borrow, to make up the sum,
And live; if no, then thou art doomed to die.
Jailer, take him to thy custody.

JAILER   I will, my lord.

EGEON
157   Hopeless and helpless doth Egeon wend,
But to procrastinate his lifeless end.   *Exeunt.*

*

✆ **I.2** *Enter Antipholus [of Syracuse], a Merchant,
and Dromio [of Syracuse].*

MERCHANT
Therefore give out you are of Epidamnum,
Lest that your goods too soon be confiscate.
This very day a Syracusian merchant
Is apprehended for arrival here,
And not being able to buy out his life,

---

144 *disannul* annul   146 *the death* the sentence of death   151 *beneficial
help* i.e., help by a benefactor   157 *wend* journey, with connotation of
death, as in "pass"
I.2 The mart in Ephesus   **s.d.** (The folios have "Antipholis Erotes," the
"Erotes" being possibly a corruption of "Erraticus," the wanderer. In II.1,
Antipholus of Ephesus is called "Sereptus," for "Surreptus," the lost or stolen
one.)

According to the statute of the town,
Dies ere the weary sun set in the west.
There is your money that I had to keep.

ANTIPHOLUS S.

Go bear it to the Centaur, where we host,   9
And stay there, Dromio, till I come to thee.   10
Within this hour it will be dinnertime;
Till that, I'll view the manners of the town,
Peruse the traders, gaze upon the buildings,
And then return and sleep within mine inn,
For with long travel I am stiff and weary.
Get thee away.

DROMIO S.

Many a man would take you at your word,
And go indeed, having so good a mean.   18

Exit Dromio [of Syracuse].

ANTIPHOLUS S.

A trusty villain, sir, that very oft,   19
When I am dull with care and melancholy,   20
Lightens my humor with his merry jests.   21
What, will you walk with me about the town,
And then go to my inn and dine with me?

MERCHANT

I am invited, sir, to certain merchants,
Of whom I hope to make much benefit;
I crave your pardon. Soon at five o'clock,   26
Please you, I'll meet with you upon the mart,
And afterward consort you till bedtime.   28
My present business calls me from you now.

---

9 *Centaur* (the name of an inn; houses, shops, and inns were identified not by numbers but by signs bearing pictures, such as that of a centaur or a phoenix) 18 *mean* means, opportunity (Dromio is a slave [who cannot "get . . . away"]) 19 *villain* person of low status (here a servant) 21 *humor* mood (in Renaissance psychology, humor was a fluid in the body, determining disposition and temperament) 26 *Soon at five o'clock* i.e., toward evening 28 *consort* accompany

ANTIPHOLUS S

30   Farewell till then. I will go lose myself,
       And wander up and down to view the city.

MERCHANT
       Sir, I commend you to your own content.   *Exit.*

ANTIPHOLUS S.
       He that commends me to mine own content,
       Commends me to the thing I cannot get.
       I to the world am like a drop of water
       That in the ocean seeks another drop,
37   Who falling there to find his fellow forth,
38   Unseen, inquisitive, confounds himself.
       So I, to find a mother and a brother,
40   In quest of them, unhappy, lose myself.
            Enter Dromio of Ephesus.
41   Here comes the almanac of my true date.
       What now? How chance thou art returned so soon?

DROMIO E.
       Returned so soon! rather approached too late.
       The capon burns, the pig falls from the spit,
45   The clock hath strucken twelve upon the bell;
       My mistress made it one upon my cheek.
       She is so hot because the meat is cold;
       The meat is cold because you come not home;
49   You come not home because you have no stomach;
50   You have no stomach, having broke your fast;
       But we, that know what 'tis to fast and pray,
52   Are penitent for your default today.

ANTIPHOLUS S.
53   Stop in your wind, sir; tell me this, I pray:
       Where have you left the money that I gave you?

---

37 *forth* out   38 *confounds himself* loses itself, mingles indistinguishably
41 *almanac* an elaborate calendar (since the two were born on the same day,
Antipholus sees the passage of time reflected in Dromio)   45 *twelve* (half an
hour late for the usual dinnertime)   49 *stomach* appetite   52 *penitent* suffering (from hunger)   53 *wind* words

DROMIO E.
　　O, sixpence, that I had o' Wednesday last
　　To pay the saddler for my mistress' crupper?   56
　　The saddler had it, sir; I kept it not.

ANTIPHOLUS S.
　　I am not in a sportive humor now.
　　Tell me, and dally not, where is the money?
　　We being strangers here, how dar'st thou trust   60
　　So great a charge from thine own custody?

DROMIO E.
　　I pray you, jest, sir, as you sit at dinner.
　　I from my mistress come to you in post;   63
　　If I return, I shall be post indeed,   64
　　For she will score your fault upon my pate.
　　Methinks your maw, like mine, should be your clock   66
　　And strike you home without a messenger.

ANTIPHOLUS S.
　　Come, Dromio, come, these jests are out of season;
　　Reserve them till a merrier hour than this.
　　Where is the gold I gave in charge to thee?   70

DROMIO E.
　　To me, sir? Why, you gave no gold to me.

ANTIPHOLUS S.
　　Come on, sir knave, have done your foolishness,
　　And tell me how thou hast disposed thy charge.

DROMIO E.
　　My charge was but to fetch you from the mart
　　Home to your house, the Phoenix, sir, to dinner;   75
　　My mistress and her sister stays for you.

ANTIPHOLUS S.
　　Now, as I am a Christian, answer me,

---

56 *crupper* strap attached to a saddle and passing under the horse's tail 63
post haste 64 *post* tavern pillar used for chalking up accounts 66 *maw*
stomach (usually applied to animals) 75 *Phoenix* i.e., the house and shop of
Antipholus of Ephesus (see I.2.9 n.)

78   In what safe place you have bestowed my money;
79   Or I shall break that merry sconce of yours
80   That stands on tricks when I am undisposed:
        Where is the thousand marks thou hadst of me?

DROMIO E.
        I have some marks of yours upon my pate,
        Some of my mistress' marks upon my shoulders,
        But not a thousand marks between you both.
        If I should pay your worship those again,
        Perchance you will not bear them patiently.

ANTIPHOLUS S.
        Thy mistress' marks? What mistress, slave, hast thou?

DROMIO E.
        Your worship's wife, my mistress at the Phoenix;
        She that doth fast till you come home to dinner,
90   And prays that you will hie you home to dinner.

ANTIPHOLUS S.
        What! wilt thou flout me thus unto my face,
        Being forbid? There, take you that, sir knave.
        [Strikes him.]

DROMIO E.
        What mean you, sir? For God's sake, hold your hands!
94   Nay, an you will not, sir, I'll take my heels.
                                Exit Dromio [of Ephesus].

ANTIPHOLUS S.
        Upon my life, by some device or other
96   The villain is o'er-raught of all my money.
97   They say this town is full of cozenage:
        As, nimble jugglers that deceive the eye,
        Dark-working sorcerers that change the mind,
100   Soul-killing witches that deform the body,
101   Disguisèd cheaters, prating mountebanks,

----

78 *bestowed* deposited   79 *sconce* head   80 *stands on* engages in   94 *an* if
96 *o'er-raught* overreached, tricked out of   97 *cozenage* cheating (Menander
and Saint Paul, among other writers, helped establish the tradition of Ephesus as a city of magic and trickery)   101 *mountebanks* charlatans (peddling
worthless wares)

And many suchlike liberties of sin: 102
If it prove so, I will be gone the sooner.
I'll to the Centaur to go seek this slave;
I greatly fear my money is not safe.   *Exit.*

*

❧ **II.1** *Enter Adriana, wife to Antipholus [of Ephesus],*
  with Luciana, her sister.

ADRIANA
  Neither my husband nor the slave returned,
  That in such haste I sent to seek his master?
  Sure, Luciana, it is two o'clock.
LUCIANA
  Perhaps some merchant hath invited him,
  And from the mart he's somewhere gone to dinner.
  Good sister, let us dine and never fret.
  A man is master of his liberty:
  Time is their master, and when they see time,
  They'll go or come; if so, be patient, sister.
ADRIANA
  Why should their liberty than ours be more?   *10*
LUCIANA
  Because their business still lies out o' door.   11
ADRIANA
  Look, when I serve him so, he takes it ill.
LUCIANA
  O, know he is the bridle of your will.   13
ADRIANA
  There's none but asses will be bridled so.
LUCIANA
  Why, headstrong liberty is lashed with woe.   15

---

102 *liberties of sin* licensed offenders (Steevens) (but the right word may be
"libertines")
    II.1 Before the house of Antipholus of Ephesus   **11** *still* always   **13** *bri-
dle* horse's bridle (but also the device used to silence and shame scolds, with a
pun on "bridal")   **15** *lashed* whipped

16 There's nothing situate under heaven's eye
    But hath his bound, in earth, in sea, in sky.
    The beasts, the fishes, and the wingèd fowls,
    Are their males' subjects, and at their controls.
20 Men, more divine, the masters of all these,
    Lords of the wide world, and wild wat'ry seas,
22 Indued with intellectual sense and souls,
    Of more preeminence than fish and fowls,
    Are masters to their females, and their lords:
    Then let your will attend on their accords.
ADRIANA
    This servitude makes you to keep unwed.
LUCIANA
    Not this, but troubles of the marriage bed.
ADRIANA
    But were you wedded, you would bear some sway.
LUCIANA
    Ere I learn love, I'll practice to obey.
ADRIANA
30 How if your husband start some otherwhere?
LUCIANA
    Till he come home again, I would forbear.
ADRIANA
    Patience unmoved! No marvel though she pause;
    They can be meek that have no other cause.
    A wretched soul, bruised with adversity,
    We bid be quiet when we hear it cry.
    But were we burdened with like weight of pain,
    As much or more we should ourselves complain:
    So thou, that hast no unkind mate to grieve thee,
39 With urging helpless patience wouldst relieve me;

16–24 *There's . . . lords* (echoing Ephesians 5, Luciana here presents the traditional idea of male supremacy in "the great chain of being")   22 *Indued*
endowed; *souls* (although this suggests that only men had souls, a belief in
women's spiritual equality often coexisted with an insistence on their social
subordination)   30 *start . . . otherwhere* i.e., turn to other women   39 *helpless* futile

But if thou live to see like right bereft,   40
This fool-begged patience in thee will be left.   41

LUCIANA
Well, I will marry one day but to try.
Here comes your man; now is your husband nigh.
   Enter Dromio of Ephesus.

ADRIANA
Say, is your tardy master now at hand?

DROMIO E.   Nay, he's at two hands with me, and that my
two ears can witness.

ADRIANA
Say, didst thou speak with him? Know'st thou his
  mind?

DROMIO E.
Ay, ay, he told his mind upon mine ear.
Beshrew his hand, I scarce could understand it.

LUCIANA   Spake he so doubtfully, thou couldst not feel   50
his meaning?

DROMIO E.   Nay, he struck so plainly, I could too well
feel his blows; and withal so doubtfully, that I could
scarce understand them.   54

ADRIANA
But say, I prithee, is he coming home?
It seems he hath great care to please his wife.

DROMIO E.
Why, mistress, sure my master is horn-mad.   57

ADRIANA
Horn-mad, thou villain!

DROMIO E.   I mean not cuckold-mad;
But, sure, he is stark mad.
When I desired him to come home to dinner,   60
He asked me for a thousand marks in gold.

---

40 *like right bereft* a similar injustice   41 *This . . . left* you will leave this foolish plea for patience   54 *understand* stand under   57 *horn-mad* acting like
an enraged horned beast (but Adriana catches first the inevitable quibble
on the horns that supposedly sprouted on cuckolds, men whose wives were
unfaithful)

"'Tis dinner time," quoth I: "My gold!" quoth he.
"Your meat doth burn," quoth I: "My gold!" quoth he.
"Will you come?" quoth I: "My gold!" quoth he –
"Where is the thousand marks I gave thee, villain?"
"The pig," quoth I, "is burned": "My gold!" quoth he.
"My mistress, sir – ," quoth I: "Hang up thy mistress!
I know not thy mistress; out on thy mistress!"

LUCIANA   Quoth who?

70 DROMIO E.   Quoth my master.
"I know," quoth he, "no house, no wife, no mistress."

72   So that my errand due unto my tongue,
I thank him, I bear home upon my shoulders;
For, in conclusion, he did beat me there.

ADRIANA
Go back again, thou slave, and fetch him home.

DROMIO E.
Go back again, and be new beaten home?
For God's sake send some other messenger.

ADRIANA
Back, slave, or I will break thy pate across.

DROMIO E.
79   And he will bless that cross with other beating.
80   Between you, I shall have a holy head.

ADRIANA
Hence, prating peasant! Fetch thy master home.

DROMIO E.
82   Am I so round with you as you with me,
That like a football you do spurn me thus?
You spurn me hence, and he will spurn me hither:
If I last in this service, you must case me in leather.

                                              [Exit.]

---

72 *due . . . tongue* which my tongue should have performed   79 *he . . . cross*
i.e., he will pay further devotion (blows) to the cross made by the blow on
my head   80 *holy* (pun on "full of holes")   82 *round* plainspoken (with pun
on usual meaning)

LUCIANA
  Fie, how impatience loureth in your face!   86
ADRIANA
  His company must do his minions grace,   87
  Whilst I at home starve for a merry look.   88
  Hath homely age th' alluring beauty took
  From my poor cheek? Then he hath wasted it.   90
  Are my discourses dull? barren my wit?
  If voluble and sharp discourse be marred,
  Unkindness blunts it more than marble hard.
  Do their gay vestments his affections bait?   94
  That's not my fault; he's master of my state.
  What ruins are in me that can be found
  By him not ruined? Then is he the ground
  Of my defeatures. My decayèd fair   98
  A sunny look of his would soon repair.
  But, too unruly deer, he breaks the pale   100
  And feeds from home; poor I am but his stale.   101
LUCIANA
  Self-harming jealousy! fie, beat it hence!
ADRIANA
  Unfeeling fools can with such wrongs dispense.   103
  I know his eye doth homage otherwhere,
  Or else what lets it but he would be here?   105
  Sister, you know he promised me a chain;
  Would that alone, a love he would detain,
  So he would keep fair quarter with his bed!   108
  I see, the jewel best enamelèd   109

---

86 *loureth* scowls 87 *minions* darlings, girlfriends 88 *starve* pine 94 *his affections bait* tempt him 98 *defeatures* disfigurements; *decayèd fair* lost beauty 100 *pale* fence 101 *from* away from; *stale* (1) a decoy or bait used in hunting, (2) a prostitute 103 *dispense* pardon (offer dispensation for) 105 *lets* prevents 108 *keep . . . bed* remain faithful in bed 109–13 *I see . . . shame* (possibly corrupt owing to omitted line or lines; the general idea seems to be that honor, like gold, is durable only up to a point, and must be guarded against wear by those who possess it)

110   Will lose his beauty; yet the gold bides still
     That others touch, and often touching will
     Wear gold; and no man that hath a name,
     By falsehood and corruption doth it shame.
     Since that my beauty cannot please his eye,
     I'll weep what's left away, and weeping die.

LUCIANA
How many fond fools serve mad jealousy!

                     Exit [with Adriana].

*

❧ **II.2** *Enter Antipholus [of Syracuse].*

ANTIPHOLUS S.
  The gold I gave to Dromio is laid up
  Safe at the Centaur; and the heedful slave
  Is wandered forth, in care to seek me out
4 By computation and mine host's report.
  I could not speak with Dromio since at first
  I sent him from the mart. See, here he comes.
    Enter Dromio of Syracuse.
  How now, sir! is your merry humor altered?
  As you love strokes, so jest with me again.
  You know no Centaur? You received no gold?
10 Your mistress sent to have me home to dinner?
  My house was at the Phoenix? Wast thou mad,
  That thus so madly thou didst answer me?

DROMIO S.
  What answer, sir? When spake I such a word?

ANTIPHOLUS S.
  Even now, even here, not half an hour since.

DROMIO S.
  I did not see you since you sent me hence,
  Home to the Centaur, with the gold you gave me.

---

110 *his* its
  II.2 A street in Ephesus   4 *computation* my reckoning

ANTIPHOLUS S.
   Villain, thou didst deny the gold's receipt,
   And told'st me of a mistress, and a dinner;
   For which, I hope, thou felt'st I was displeased.
DROMIO S.
   I am glad to see you in this merry vein.   20
   What means this jest? I pray you, master, tell me.
ANTIPHOLUS S.
   Yea, dost thou jeer and flout me in the teeth?   22
   Think'st thou I jest? Hold, take thou that, and that.
      Beats Dromio.
DROMIO S.
   Hold, sir, for God's sake! Now your jest is earnest.   24
   Upon what bargain do you give it me?
ANTIPHOLUS S.
   Because that I familiarly sometimes
   Do use you for my fool, and chat with you,
   Your sauciness will jest upon my love,
   And make a common of my serious hours.   29
   When the sun shines let foolish gnats make sport,   30
   But creep in crannies when he hides his beams.
   If you will jest with me, know my aspect,   32
   And fashion your demeanor to my looks,
   Or I will beat this method in your sconce.   34
DROMIO S.   Sconce, call you it? So you would leave bat-
   tering, I had rather have it a head. An you use these   36
   blows long, I must get a sconce for my head and en-   37
   sconce it too; or else I shall seek my wit in my shoul-   38
   ders. But I pray, sir, why am I beaten?
ANTIPHOLUS S.   Dost thou not know?   40

---

22 *in the teeth* to my face   24 *earnest* (1) serious, (2) down payment to se-
cure a bargain (see l. 25)   29 *common* public land, open to all comers   32
know . . . aspect read my face (Antipholus imparts traditional advice that servants and wives should mirror their masters' moods and conduct)   34–37
sconce head; fort; helmet   36 *An* if   37 *ensconce* protect militarily   38–39
seek . . . shoulders (because his brains will have been beaten out)

DROMIO S. Nothing, sir, but that I am beaten.

ANTIPHOLUS S. Shall I tell you why?

DROMIO S. Ay, sir, and wherefore; for they say every why hath a wherefore.

ANTIPHOLUS S. Why, first – for flouting me; and then, wherefore – for urging it the second time to me.

DROMIO S.
Was there ever any man thus beaten out of season,
When in the why and the wherefore is neither rhyme
    nor reason?
Well, sir, I thank you.

50 ANTIPHOLUS S. Thank me, sir, for what?

DROMIO S. Marry, sir, for this something that you gave me for nothing.

ANTIPHOLUS S. I'll make you amends next, to give you nothing for something. But say, sir, is it dinnertime?

55 DROMIO S. No, sir, I think the meat wants that I have.

56 ANTIPHOLUS S. In good time, sir; what's that?

57 DROMIO S. Basting.

ANTIPHOLUS S. Well, sir, then 'twill be dry.

DROMIO S. If it be, sir, I pray you eat none of it.

60 ANTIPHOLUS S. Your reason?

61 DROMIO S. Lest it make you choleric, and purchase me
62 another dry basting.

ANTIPHOLUS S. Well, sir, learn to jest in good time. There's a time for all things.

DROMIO S. I durst have denied that, before you were so choleric.

ANTIPHOLUS S. By what rule, sir?

68 DROMIO S. Marry, sir, by a rule as plain as the plain bald pate of Father Time himself.

---

55 *wants . . . have* lacks what I have   56 *In good time* indeed   57 *Basting* moistening with pan juices (but also beating)   61 *choleric* overcome by choler (one of the four "humors" thought to be in balance in the healthy body, and therefore ill-tempered, angry)   62 *dry basting* hard beating (properly, not drawing blood)   68 *Marry* by the Virgin Mary (grown to be only a mild oath)

ANTIPHOLUS S.   Let's hear it.   70

DROMIO S.   There's no time for a man to recover his hair
that grows bald by nature.

ANTIPHOLUS S.   May he not do it by fine and recovery?   73

DROMIO S.   Yes, to pay a fine for a periwig and recover
the lost hair of another man.

ANTIPHOLUS S.   Why is Time such a niggard of hair,
being, as it is, so plentiful an excrement?   77

DROMIO S.   Because it is a blessing that he bestows on
beasts; and what he hath scanted men in hair, he hath
given them in wit.   80

ANTIPHOLUS S.   Why, but there's many a man hath more
hair than wit.

DROMIO S.   Not a man of those but he hath the wit to
lose his hair.

ANTIPHOLUS S.   Why, thou didst conclude hairy men
plain dealers without wit.

DROMIO S.   The plainer dealer, the sooner lost; yet he   87
loseth it in a kind of jollity.

ANTIPHOLUS S.   For what reason?

DROMIO S.   For two; and sound ones too.   90

ANTIPHOLUS S.   Nay, not sound, I pray you.   91

DROMIO S.   Sure ones, then.

ANTIPHOLUS S.   Nay, not sure, in a thing falsing.

DROMIO S.   Certain ones, then.

ANTIPHOLUS S.   Name them.

DROMIO S.   The one, to save the money that he spends in
tiring; the other, that at dinner they should not drop in   97
his porridge.

ANTIPHOLUS S.   You would all this time have proved,
there is no time for all things.   100

---

73 *fine and recovery* (quibble on legal procedure for gaining absolute owner-
ship)   77 *excrement* (something, like hair, that grows from the body)   87–
88 *The . . . jollity* (alluding to loss of hair from sexually transmitted disease)
90–91 *sound, sound* valid; free of disease   97 *tiring* dressing (the hair)

DROMIO S   Marry, and did, sir; namely, no time to recover hair lost by nature.

ANTIPHOLUS S.   But your reason was not substantial, why
there is no time to recover.

DROMIO S.   Thus I mend it: Time himself is bald, and
106   therefore to the world's end will have bald followers.

ANTIPHOLUS S.   I knew 'twould be a bald conclusion. But
soft! who wafts us yonder?
       Enter Adriana and Luciana.

ADRIANA

109   Ay, ay, Antipholus, look strange and frown.
110   Some other mistress hath thy sweet aspects;
I am not Adriana, nor thy wife.
The time was once when thou unurged wouldst vow
That never words were music to thine ear,
That never object pleasing in thine eye,
That never touch well welcome to thy hand,
That never meat sweet-savored in thy taste,
Unless I spake, or looked, or touched, or carved to thee.
How comes it now, my husband, O, how comes it,
That thou art then estrangèd from thyself?
120   Thyself I call it, being strange to me,
That, undividable, incorporate,
Am better than thy dear self's better part.
Ah, do not tear away thyself from me!
124   For know, my love, as easy mayst thou fall
A drop of water in the breaking gulf,
And take unmingled thence that drop again
Without addition or diminishing,
As take from me thyself and not me too.
How dearly would it touch thee to the quick,
130   Shouldst thou but hear I were licentious,

---

106 *bald* paltry, lame (besides the continued reference to the head) **109**
strange estranged (cf. ll. 119, 120)   **110** *aspects* countenance (cf. l. 32)   **124**
fall let fall

And that this body, consecrate to thee,
By ruffian lust should be contaminate!
Wouldst thou not spit at me, and spurn at me,   133
And hurl the name of husband in my face,
And tear the stained skin off my harlot brow,
And from my false hand cut the wedding ring,
And break it with a deep-divorcing vow?
I know thou canst, and therefore see thou do it.
I am possessed with an adulterate blot;   139
My blood is mingled with the crime of lust.   *140*
For if we two be one, and thou play false,
I do digest the poison of thy flesh,
Being strumpeted by thy contagion.
Keep then fair league and truce with thy true bed;
I live distained, thou undishonorèd.   145

ANTIPHOLUS S.
Plead you to me, fair dame? I know you not.
In Ephesus I am but two hours old,
As strange unto your town as to your talk;
Who every word by all my wit being scanned,
Wants wit in all, one word to understand.   *150*

LUCIANA
Fie, brother! how the world is changed with you!
When were you wont to use my sister thus?
She sent for you by Dromio home to dinner.

ANTIPHOLUS S.   By Dromio?

DROMIO S.   By me?

ADRIANA
By thee; and this thou didst return from him,
That he did buffet thee, and in his blows,
Denied my house for his, me for his wife.

---

133 *spurn at* trip, kick, scorn   139–45 (building on the conceit that husband and wife are "one flesh," Adriana claims that her husband's adultery is itself a sexually transmitted disease, a contagious shame in which she shares) 145 *distained* unstained (by contagion)

ANTIPHOLUS S.

    Did you converse, sir, with this gentlewoman?

160   What is the course and drift of your compact?

DROMIO S.

    I, sir? I never saw her till this time.

ANTIPHOLUS S.

    Villain, thou liest; for even her very words

    Didst thou deliver to me on the mart.

DROMIO S.

    I never spake with her in all my life.

ANTIPHOLUS S.

    How can she thus then call us by our names?

    Unless it be by inspiration.

ADRIANA

    How ill agrees it with your gravity

    To counterfeit thus grossly with your slave,

    Abetting him to thwart me in my mood!

170   Be it my wrong you are from me exempt,

    But wrong not that wrong with a more contempt.

    Come, I will fasten on this sleeve of thine:

    Thou art an elm, my husband, I a vine,

    Whose weakness married to thy stronger state

    Makes me with thy strength to communicate.

176   If aught possess thee from me, it is dross,

177   Usurping ivy, brier, or idle moss;

    Who all for want of pruning, with intrusion

179   Infect thy sap and live on thy confusion.

ANTIPHOLUS S.

180   To me she speaks; she moves me for her theme.

    What, was I married to her in my dream?

    Or sleep I now, and think I hear all this?

183   What error drives our eyes and ears amiss?

---

160 *compact* conspiracy 170 *exempt* cut off 176 *possess* take 177 *idle* worthless 179 *confusion* destruction 180 *moves* appeals to 183 *error* (here, as elsewhere in the play, the word suggests the uncanny illusions of Ephesus; cf. ll. 188–89)

Until I know this sure uncertainty,
I'll entertain the offered fallacy.   185
LUCIANA
Dromio, go bid the servants spread for dinner.
DROMIO S.
O, for my beads! I cross me for a sinner.   187
This is the fairyland. O spite of spites,
We talk with goblins, owls, and sprites!
If we obey them not, this will ensue: 190
They'll suck our breath, or pinch us black and blue.
LUCIANA
Why prat'st thou to thyself and answer'st not?
Dromio, thou drone, thou snail, thou slug, thou sot!
DROMIO S.
I am transformèd, master, am I not?
ANTIPHOLUS S.
I think thou art, in mind, and so am I.
DROMIO S.
Nay, master, both in mind and in my shape.
ANTIPHOLUS S.
Thou hast thine own form.   No, I am an ape.
DROMIO S.
LUCIANA
If thou art changed to aught, 'tis to an ass.
DROMIO S.
'Tis true; she rides me, and I long for grass.   199
'Tis so, I am an ass; else it could never be   200
But I should know her as well as she knows me.
ADRIANA
Come, come, no longer will I be a fool,
To put the finger in the eye and weep,
Whilst man and master laughs my woes to scorn.
Come, sir, to dinner. Dromio, keep the gate.

---

185 *entertain . . . fallacy* accept what seems to be true   187 *beads* rosary
199 *rides* (with the sexual meaning of mounting; she is a woman on top);
grass grazing (possibly freedom or release)

206   Husband, I'll dine above with you today,
207   And shrive you of a thousand idle pranks.
208   Sirrah, if any ask you for your master,
       Say he dines forth, and let no creature enter.
210   Come, sister. Dromio, play the porter well.

ANTIPHOLUS S.
       Am I in earth, in heaven, or in hell?
212   Sleeping or waking? mad or well advised?
       Known unto these, and to myself disguised!
       I'll say as they say, and persever so,
       And in this mist at all adventures go.

DROMIO S.
       Master, shall I be porter at the gate?

ADRIANA
       Ay; and let none enter, lest I break your pate.

LUCIANA
       Come, come, Antipholus, we dine too late.   *[Exeunt.]*

                  *

∾ **III.1** *Enter Antipholus of Ephesus, his man Dromio,*
    Angelo the Goldsmith, and Balthasar the Merchant.

ANTIPHOLUS E.
       Good Signor Angelo, you must excuse us all;
       My wife is shrewish when I keep not hours.
       Say that I lingered with you at your shop
4   To see the making of her carcanet,
       And that tomorrow you will bring it home.
6   But here's a villain that would face me down

---

206 *dine above* (The dinner would presumably be seen "above" – i.e., on the upper stage. In Elizabethan homes the living quarters were on an upper floor, while the place of business was on the ground level.) 207 *shrive you* hear your confession 208 *Sirrah* (term of address for servants and other social inferiors) 212 *well advised* sane
    III.1 Before the house of Antipholus of Ephesus 4 *carcanet* necklace of gold or set with jewels 6 *face me down* outface me (with the assertion that)

He met me on the mart, and that I beat him,
And charged him with a thousand marks in gold,
And that I did deny my wife and house.   9
Thou drunkard, thou, what didst thou mean by this?   10

DROMIO E.
Say what you will, sir, but I know what I know;
That you beat me at the mart, I have your hand to   12
   show.
If the skin were parchment and the blows you gave
   were ink,
Your own handwriting would tell you what I think.

ANTIPHOLUS E.
I think thou art an ass.

DROMIO E.   Marry, so it doth appear
By the wrongs I suffer and the blows I bear.
I should kick, being kicked; and, being at that pass,   17
You would keep from my heels and beware of an ass.

ANTIPHOLUS E.
You're sad, Signor Balthasar. Pray God, our cheer   19
May answer my good will and your good welcome   20
   here.

BALTHASAR
I hold your dainties cheap, sir, and your welcome dear.   21

ANTIPHOLUS E.
O, Signor Balthasar, either at flesh or fish,
A tableful of welcome makes scarce one dainty dish.

BALTHASAR
Good meat, sir, is common; that every churl affords.   24

ANTIPHOLUS E.
And welcome more common, for that's nothing but
   words.

---

9 *deny* disclaim   12 *hand* handiwork (on my body; "hand" could also mean handwriting)   17 *at that pass* in that direction   19 *sad* serious (its usual meaning in Shakespeare); *cheer* hospitality   20 *answer* correspond to   21 *dainties* delicacies   24 *churl* person of lowest rank

BALTHASAR
  Small cheer and great welcome makes a merry feast.
ANTIPHOLUS E.
  Ay, to a niggardly host and more sparing guest.
28 But though my cates be mean, take them in good part;
  Better cheer may you have, but not with better heart.
30 But soft! my door is locked. Go bid them let us in.
DROMIO E.
  Maud, Bridget, Marian, Cicely, Gillian, Ginn!
DROMIO S. *[Within]*
32 Mome, malt horse, capon, coxcomb, idiot, patch!
33 Either get thee from the door or sit down at the hatch.
34 Dost thou conjure for wenches, that thou call'st for
    such store,
  When one is one too many? Go get thee from the
    door.
DROMIO E.
  What patch is made our porter? My master stays in
    the street.
DROMIO S. *[Within]*
  Let him walk from whence he came, lest he catch cold
  on's feet.
ANTIPHOLUS E.
  Who talks within there? Ho, open the door!
DROMIO S. *[Within]*
  Right, sir; I'll tell you when, an you'll tell me where-
    fore.
ANTIPHOLUS E.
40 Wherefore? For my dinner: I have not dined today.
DROMIO S.
  Nor today here you must not; come again when you
  may.

---

28 *cates* delicacies; *mean* plain **32** *Mome, patch* (both words mean "fool")
33 *hatch* half door; gate or wicket with an open space above **34** *conjure for*
bring into being by magic; *store* quantity (of wenches)

ANTIPHOLUS E.

    What art thou that keep'st me out from the house I   42
    owe?

DROMIO S.   *[Within]*

    The porter for this time, sir, and my name is Dromio.

DROMIO E.

    O villain, thou hast stol'n both mine office and my
    name!

    The one ne'er got me credit, the other mickle blame.   45

    If thou hadst been Dromio today in my place,

    Thou wouldst have changed thy face for a name, or   47
    thy name for an ass.

    Enter Luce [within].

LUCE   *[Within]*

    What a coil is there, Dromio! Who are those at the   48
    gate?

DROMIO E.

    Let my master in, Luce.

LUCE   *[Within]*   Faith, no; he comes too late;

    And so tell your master.   50

DROMIO E.   O Lord, I must laugh!

    Have at you with a proverb: Shall I set in my staff?   51

LUCE   *[Within]*

    Have at you with another: that's – When? Can you   52
    tell?

DROMIO S.   *[Within]*

    If thy name be called Luce – Luce, thou hast answered
    him well.

---

42 *owe* own (frequent meaning)   **45** *mickle* much   **47** *Thou . . . ass* (obscure; Dromio E. may mean that the name brought his face into trouble, so that, with the beatings, an ass would have been more appropriate)   **48** *Who . . . gate* (both Luce and Adriana are on the upper stage and hence unable to see Antipholus E. and Dromio E., who are by the rear door under the balcony)   **51** *Have . . . proverb* I'll throw a proverb at you; *set . . . staff* claim my home   **52** *When . . . tell* (another proverb, used to evade a question)

ANTIPHOLUS E.

54   Do you hear, you minion? You'll let us in, I hope?

LUCE   *[Within]*

   I thought to have asked you.

DROMIO S.   *[Within]*   And you said no.

DROMIO E.

   So come, help: well struck! There was blow for blow.

ANTIPHOLUS E.

   Thou baggage, let me in.

LUCE   *[Within]*   Can you tell for whose sake?

DROMIO E.

   Master, knock the door hard.

LUCE   *[Within]*   Let him knock till it ache.

ANTIPHOLUS E.

   You'll cry for this, minion, if I beat the door down.

LUCE   *[Within]*

60   What needs all that, and a pair of stocks in the town?

    Enter Adriana [Within].

ADRIANA   *[Within]*

   Who is that at the door that keeps all this noise?

DROMIO S.   *[Within]*

   By my troth, your town is troubled with unruly boys.

ANTIPHOLUS E.

   Are you there, wife? You might have come before.

ADRIANA   *[Within]*

   Your wife, sir knave! Go get you from the door.

DROMIO E.

   If you went in pain, master, this "knave" would go sore.

ANGELO

   Here is neither cheer, sir, nor welcome; we would fain
   have either.

---

54 *minion* hussy   60 *What . . . town* why should we be pestered with these
rowdies when the town has stocks (an engine of punishment, in which the
offender would sit with his or her ankles secured between two boards, ex-
posed to public humiliation and abuse)

BALTHASAR
    In debating which was best, we shall part with neither.
DROMIO E.
    They stand at the door, master; bid them welcome
        hither.
ANTIPHOLUS E.
    There is something in the wind, that we cannot get in.
DROMIO E.
    You would say so, master, if your garments were thin.   70
    Your cake here is warm within; you stand here in the
        cold.
    It would make a man mad as a buck to be so bought   72
        and sold.
ANTIPHOLUS E.
    Go fetch me something; I'll break ope the gate.
DROMIO S.   [Within]
    Break any breaking here, and I'll break your knave's
        pate.
DROMIO E.
    A man may break a word with you, sir, and words are
        but wind:
    Ay, and break it in your face, so he break it not be-
        hind.
DROMIO S.   [Within]
    It seems thou want'st breaking. Out upon thee, hind!   77
DROMIO E.
    Here's too much "Out upon thee!" I pray thee, let me
        in.
DROMIO S.   [Within]
    Ay, when fowls have no feathers, and fish have no fin.
ANTIPHOLUS E.
    Well, I'll break in. Go borrow me a crow.   80

---

72 *mad as a buck* i.e., in mating season; *bought and sold* used (This suggests
that Adriana may have a substitute in her bed as well as at her table, as in
Plautus's *Amphitruo*.)   77 *hind* servant   80 *crow* crowbar

DROMIO E.
   A crow without feather? Master, mean you so?
   For a fish without a fin, there's a fowl without a
      feather:
83   If a crow help us in, sirrah, we'll pluck a crow together.
ANTIPHOLUS E.
   Go get thee gone; fetch me an iron crow.
BALTHASAR
   Have patience, sir; O let it not be so!
   Herein you war against your reputation,
87   And draw within the compass of suspect
   Th' unviolated honor of your wife.
89   Once this – your long experience of her wisdom,
90   Her sober virtue, years, and modesty,
   Plead on her part some cause to you unknown;
92   And doubt not, sir, but she will well excuse
93   Why at this time the doors are made against you.
   Be ruled by me: depart in patience,
   And let us to the Tiger all to dinner;
   And about evening come yourself alone,
   To know the reason of this strange restraint.
98   If by strong hand you offer to break in
99   Now in the stirring passage of the day,
100   A vulgar comment will be made of it,
   And that supposèd by the common rout
102   Against your yet ungallèd estimation,
   That may with foul intrusion enter in
   And dwell upon your grave when you are dead;
105   For slander lives upon succession,
   Forever housed where it gets possession.

---

83 *pluck a crow* pick a bone, settle accounts   87 *draw . . . suspect* bring under suspicion   89 *Once this* give one thought to this   92 *excuse* explain
93 *made* shut   98 *offer* try   99 *stirring passage* bustle   100 *vulgar* by "the
common rout" (next line; not usually "cheap")   102 *yet . . . estimation* hitherto untouched reputation   105 *slander . . . succession* one slander takes over
from the preceding one and, in turn, breeds more

ANTIPHOLUS E.
    You have prevailed: I will depart in quiet,
    And in despite of mirth mean to be merry.   108
    I know a wench of excellent discourse,
    Pretty and witty, wild and yet, too, gentle.   110
    There will we dine. This woman that I mean,
    My wife – but, I protest, without desert –   112
    Hath oftentimes upbraided me withal:
    To her will we to dinner. *[To Angelo]* Get you home
    And fetch the chain; by this I know 'tis made.   115
    Bring it, I pray you, to the Porpentine;   116
    For there's the house. That chain will I bestow,
    Be it for nothing but to spite my wife,
    Upon mine hostess there. Good sir, make haste.
    Since mine own doors refuse to entertain me,   120
    I'll knock elsewhere, to see if they'll disdain me.
ANGELO
    I'll meet you at that place some hour hence.
ANTIPHOLUS E.
    Do so. This jest shall cost me some expense.   *Exeunt.*

*

❧ **III.2** *Enter Luciana, with Antipholus of Syracuse.*

LUCIANA
    And may it be that you have quite forgot
    A husband's office? Shall, Antipholus,
    Even in the spring of love, thy love-springs rot?   3
    Shall love, in building, grow so ruinous?
    If you did wed my sister for her wealth,
    Then for her wealth's sake use her with more kindness:
    Or if you like elsewhere, do it by stealth;

---

108 *in . . . mirth* despite mockery (?)   112 *without desert* unjustly   115 *by this* by this time   116 *Porpentine* Porcupine (here the name of an inn)
    III.2 The same   3 *love-springs* love-shoots (as of a young plant)

Muffle your false love with some show of blindness:
Let not my sister read it in your eye;
10 Be not thy tongue thy own shame's orator;
11 Look sweet, speak fair, become disloyalty;
12 Apparel vice like virtue's harbinger;
Bear a fair presence, though your heart be tainted;
14 Teach sin the carriage of a holy saint;
Be secret-false: what need she be acquainted?
16 What simple thief brags of his own attaint?
'Tis double wrong to truant with your bed,
18 And let her read it in thy looks at board.
19 Shame hath a bastard fame, well managèd;
20 Ill deeds is doubled with an evil word.
Alas, poor women! make us but believe,
22 Being compact of credit, that you love us;
Though others have the arm, show us the sleeve;
24 We in your motion turn, and you may move us.
Then, gentle brother, get you in again;
Comfort my sister, cheer her, call her wife.
27 'Tis holy sport to be a little vain,
When the sweet breath of flattery conquers strife.

ANTIPHOLUS 3.
Sweet mistress – what your name is else, I know not,
30 Nor by what wonder you do hit of mine –
Less in your knowledge and your grace you show not
32 Than our earth's wonder; more than earth divine.
Teach me, dear creature, how to think and speak;
34 Lay open to my earthy-gross conceit,
Smothered in errors, feeble, shallow, weak,
36 The folded meaning of your words' deceit.

---

10 *orator* advocate   11 *become disloyalty* make disloyalty seem becoming (attractive)   12 *harbinger* herald, advance messenger to a court   14 *carriage*
manners   16 *attaint* disgrace, crime   18 *board* table   19 *bastard fame* coun-
terfeit reputation   22 *compact of credit* composed of trust – i.e., made so that
(we) will believe anything   24 *We . . . turn* our moves are governed by yours
27 *vain* false   30 *hit of* hit upon   32 *our earth's wonder* Elizabeth I (?)   34
earthy-gross conceit wit gross as earth   36 *folded* i.e., so as to be concealed

Against my soul's pure truth why labor you
To make it wander in an unknown field?
Are you a god? Would you create me new?
Transform me then, and to your power I'll yield.   40
But if that I am I, then well I know
Your weeping sister is no wife of mine,
Nor to her bed no homage do I owe.
Far more, far more, to you do I decline.   44
O train me not, sweet mermaid, with thy note,   45
To drown me in thy sister's flood of tears!
Sing, siren, for thyself, and I will dote.
Spread o'er the silver waves thy golden hairs,
And as a bed I'll take them and there lie;
And in that glorious supposition think   50
He gains by death that hath such means to die.
Let Love, being light, be drownèd if she sink!   52

LUCIANA
What, are you mad, that you do reason so?

ANTIPHOLUS S.
Not mad, but mated; how, I do not know.   54

LUCIANA
It is a fault that springeth from your eye.

ANTIPHOLUS S.
For gazing on your beams, fair sun, being by.

LUCIANA
Gaze where you should, and that will clear your sight.

ANTIPHOLUS S.
As good to wink, sweet love, as look on night.   58

LUCIANA
Why call you me love? Call my sister so.

ANTIPHOLUS S.
Thy sister's sister.   60

LUCIANA   That's my sister.

---

44 *decline* incline   45 *train* entice; *note* music   52 *light* (1) light in weight,
(2) wanton   54 *mated* (1) amazed, (2) confounded, (3) defeated, (4) married   58 *wink* close the eyes (usual meaning in Shakespeare)

ANTIPHOLUS S.   No;
   It is thyself, mine own self's better part;
   Mine eye's clear eye, my dear heart's dearer heart;
   My food, my fortune, and my sweet hope's aim;
64   My sole earth's heaven, and my heaven's claim.

LUCIANA
   All this my sister is, or else should be.

ANTIPHOLUS S.
66   Call thyself sister, sweet, for I am thee.
   Thee will I love, and with thee lead my life;
   Thou hast no husband yet, nor I no wife.
   Give me thy hand.

LUCIANA   O, soft, sir! hold you still.
70   I'll fetch my sister, to get her good will.   *Exit.*
   Enter Dromio of Syracuse.

ANTIPHOLUS S.   Why, how now, Dromio! Where runn'st
thou so fast?

DROMIO S.   Do you know me, sir? Am I Dromio? Am I
your man? Am I myself?

ANTIPHOLUS S.   Thou art Dromio, thou art my man,
thou art thyself.

DROMIO S.   I am an ass, I am a woman's man, and besides myself.

ANTIPHOLUS S.   What woman's man? and how besides
80   thyself?

DROMIO S.   Marry, sir, besides myself, I am due to a
woman: one that claims me, one that haunts me, one
that will have me.

ANTIPHOLUS S.   What claim lays she to thee?

DROMIO S.   Marry, sir, such claim as you would lay to
86   your horse; and she would have me as a beast: not that,

---

64 *My . . . claim* my only heaven on earth, and my claim given me by (or to)
heaven 66 *am* (often emended to "aim" – unnecessarily, in view of l. 61)
86 *a beast* (pun on "abased," since "beast" was pronounced "baste"; Dromio
suggests that sex with Luce/Nell would be a kind of bestiality)

I being a beast, she would have me; but that she, being
a very beastly creature, lays claim to me.

ANTIPHOLUS S.   What is she?

DROMIO S.   A very reverent body; aye, such a one as a   90
man may not speak of, without he say, "Sir-reverence."   91
I have but lean luck in the match, and yet is she a won-   92
drous fat marriage.

ANTIPHOLUS S.   How dost thou mean a fat marriage?

DROMIO S.   Marry, sir, she's the kitchen wench, and all
grease; and I know not what use to put her to, but to   96
make a lamp of her, and run from her by her own light.
I warrant, her rags and the tallow in them will burn a
Poland winter. If she lives till doomsday, she'll burn a
week longer than the whole world.   100

ANTIPHOLUS S.   What complexion is she of?

DROMIO S.   Swart, like my shoe, but her face nothing   102
like so clean kept; for why? She sweats; a man may go   103
over shoes in the grime of it.

ANTIPHOLUS S.   That's a fault that water will mend.

DROMIO S.   No, sir, 'tis in grain; Noah's flood could not   106
do it.

ANTIPHOLUS S.   What's her name?

DROMIO S.   Nell, sir; but her name and three quarters –   109
that's an ell and three quarters – will not measure her   110
from hip to hip.

ANTIPHOLUS S.   Then she bears some breadth?

---

91 *Sir-reverence* if you will pardon the expression (corruption of "saving reverence")   92 *lean* poor, scanty (besides the obvious contrast with *fat*)   96
grease (another bad pun, "grease" being pronounced "grace")   102 *Swart*
dark, black   103 *for why?* (the question mark in the folio text may be un-
necessary, since "for why" meant "because")   106 *in grain* fast dyed, in-
grained   109 *Nell* (hitherto called Luce)   110 *ell* forty-five inches (Nell
bears some breadth – almost seven feet in circumference)

DROMIO S.   No longer from head to foot than from hip
to hip: she is spherical, like a globe; I could find out
115   countries in her.

ANTIPHOLUS S.   In what part of her body stands Ireland?

DROMIO S.   Marry, sir, in her buttocks. I found it out by
the bogs.

ANTIPHOLUS S.   Where Scotland?

120   DROMIO S.   I found it by the barrenness; hard in the
palm of the hand.

122   ANTIPHOLUS S.   Where France?

DROMIO S.   In her forehead, armed and reverted, making
war against her heir.

ANTIPHOLUS S.   Where England?

DROMIO S.   I looked for the chalky cliffs, but I could find
127   no whiteness in them; but I guess it stood in her chin,
by the salt rheum that ran between France and it.

ANTIPHOLUS S.   Where Spain?

130   DROMIO S.   Faith, I saw it not; but I felt it hot in her
breath.

ANTIPHOLUS S.   Where America, the Indies?

133   DROMIO S.   O, sir, upon her nose, all o'er embellished
134   with rubies, carbuncles, sapphires, declining their rich
135   aspect to the hot breath of Spain, who sent whole
136   armadoes of carracks to be ballast at her nose.

137   ANTIPHOLUS S.   Where stood Belgia, the Netherlands?

115–37 *countries in her* (This conventional mapping of the female body was
sometimes done reverently, as in Donne's Elegy 19 ["O my America! my
new-found land"], sometimes derisively, as here. Conversely, land might be
described as a female body, as in Ralegh's notorious claim that Guiana was a
"countrey that hath yet her maydenhead." This passage also belongs to the
tradition of cataloguing women's attributes, positively [blazon] or negatively
[anti-blazon].)   122–24 *France . . . heir* (often seen as a reference to the
French Civil War [c. 1589–93], and thus as a clue to dating the play; the
claim that Luce/Nell's hairline is receding may also suggest that she has had a
sexually transmitted disease)   127 *them* i.e., Nell's teeth   134–35 *declining . . . aspect* looking downward   136 *armadoes of carracks* armadas of great
merchant ships or galleons (a topical allusion, suggesting that the date of the
play was not much later than 1588); *ballast* freighted   137 *Belgia, the
Netherlands* (usually called the Low Countries)

DROMIO S.   O, sir! I did not look so low. To conclude,
   this drudge, or diviner, laid claim to me; called me   139
   Dromio; swore I was assured to her; told me what privy 140
   marks I had about me, as the mark of my shoulder, the
   mole in my neck, the great wart on my left arm, that I,
   amazed, ran from her as a witch.
   And I think, if my breast had not been made of faith,   144
     and my heart of steel,
   She had transformed me to a curtal dog, and made me   145
     turn i' the wheel.

ANTIPHOLUS S.
   Go hie thee presently post to the road;   146
   And if the wind blow any way from shore,   147
   I will not harbor in this town tonight.
   If any bark put forth, come to the mart,
   Where I will walk till thou return to me.   150
   If everyone knows us, and we know none,
   'Tis time, I think, to trudge, pack, and be gone.

DROMIO S.
   As from a bear a man would run for life,
   So fly I from her that would be my wife.   *Exit.*

ANTIPHOLUS S.
   There's none but witches do inhabit here,
   And therefore 'tis high time that I were hence.
   She that doth call me husband, even my soul
   Doth for a wife abhor. But her fair sister,
   Possessed with such a gentle sovereign grace,
   Of such enchanting presence and discourse,   160
   Hath almost made me traitor to myself.
   But lest myself be guilty to self-wrong,
   I'll stop mine ears against the mermaid's song.

---

139 *diviner* witch, with powers of prophecy 140 *assured* betrothed 145
curtal with shortened tail (hence of no value in hunting); *turn i' the wheel*
(dogs were said to be very good at turning the cooking spits) 146 *hie* hurry;
presently at once; *post* in haste; *road* roadstead or harbor 147 *And if* if

Enter Angelo with the chain.

ANGELO   Master Antipholus –

ANTIPHOLUS S.   Ay, that's my name.

ANGELO

I know it well, sir; lo, here is the chain.

I thought to have ta'en you at the Porpentine;

The chain unfinished made me stay thus long.

ANTIPHOLUS S.

What is your will that I shall do with this?

ANGELO

170   What please yourself, sir; I have made it for you.

ANTIPHOLUS S.

171   Made it for me, sir! I bespoke it not.

ANGELO

Not once, nor twice, but twenty times you have.

Go home with it and please your wife withal;

And soon at suppertime I'll visit you,

And then receive my money for the chain.

ANTIPHOLUS S.

I pray you, sir, receive the money now,

For fear you ne'er see chain nor money more.

ANGELO

You are a merry man, sir; fare you well.   *Exit.*

ANTIPHOLUS S.

What I should think of this, I cannot tell;

180   But this I think, there's no man is so vain

That would refuse so fair an offered chain.

182   I see a man here needs not live by shifts,

When in the streets he meets such golden gifts.

I'll to the mart, and there for Dromio stay;

185   If any ship put out, then straight away.   *Exit.*

*

---

171 *bespoke* ordered   180 *vain* foolish   182 *shifts* tricks   185 *straight* directly

❧ **IV.1** *Enter a [Second] Merchant, [Angelo the]*
Goldsmith, and an Officer.

SECOND MERCHANT
  You know since Pentecost the sum is due,
  And since I have not much importuned you;
  Nor now I had not, but that I am bound
  To Persia, and want guilders for my voyage.
  Therefore make present satisfaction,
  Or I'll attach you by this officer.   6
ANGELO
  Even just the sum that I do owe to you
  Is growing to me by Antipholus;   8
  And in the instant that I met with you
  He had of me a chain. At five o'clock   10
  I shall receive the money for the same.
  Pleaseth you walk with me down to his house,
  I will discharge my bond, and thank you too.
      Enter Antipholus [of] Ephesus [and] Dromio [of
      Ephesus] from the Courtesan's.
OFFICER
  That labor may you save; see where he comes.
ANTIPHOLUS E.
  While I go to the goldsmith's house, go thou
  And buy a rope's end; that will I bestow
  Among my wife and her confederates,
  For locking me out of my doors by day.
  But soft! I see the goldsmith. Get thee gone;
  Buy thou a rope, and bring it home to me.   20

IV.1 A street in Ephesus 1 *Pentecost* (Christian holiday, seventh Sunday
after Easter) 6 *attach* arrest (holding the debtor as collateral for the debt
was standard practice) 8 *growing* accruing

DROMIO E.

21   I buy a thousand pounds a year! I buy a rope!

> *Exit Dromio [of Ephesus].*

ANTIPHOLUS E.

22   A man is well holp up that trusts to you.
      I promisèd your presence and the chain;
      But neither chain nor goldsmith came to me.
      Belike you thought our love would last too long
      If it were chained together, and therefore came not.

ANGELO

      Saving your merry humor, here's the note
      How much your chain weighs to the utmost carat,
29   The fineness of the gold, and chargeful fashion,
30   Which doth amount to three odd ducats more
      Than I stand debted to this gentleman.
      I pray you see him presently discharged,
      For he is bound to sea and stays but for it.

ANTIPHOLUS E.

      I am not furnished with the present money;
      Besides, I have some business in the town.
      Good signor, take the stranger to my house,
      And with you take the chain, and bid my wife
      Disburse the sum on the receipt thereof.
      Perchance I will be there as soon as you.

ANGELO

40   Then you will bring the chain to her yourself?

ANTIPHOLUS E.

      No; bear it with you, lest I come not time enough.

ANGELO

      Well, sir, I will. Have you the chain about you?

ANTIPHOLUS E.

43   An if I have not, sir, I hope you have,
      Or else you may return without your money.

---

21 *I . . . rope* (a puzzling line; perhaps Dromio thinks of the rope as an in-
strument that his master will use to beat or "pound" him)   22 *holp* helped
29 *chargeful* costly   43 *An if* if

ANGELO
  Nay, come, I pray you, sir, give me the chain.
  Both wind and tide stays for this gentleman,
  And I, to blame, have held him here too long.

ANTIPHOLUS E.
  Good Lord! you use this dalliance to excuse   48
  Your breach of promise to the Porpentine.
  I should have chid you for not bringing it,   50
  But, like a shrew, you first begin to brawl.

SECOND MERCHANT
  The hour steals on; I pray you, sir, dispatch.

ANGELO
  You hear how he importunes me: the chain!

ANTIPHOLUS E.
  Why, give it to my wife and fetch your money.

ANGELO
  Come, come, you know I gave it you even now.
  Either send the chain or send me by some token.   56

ANTIPHOLUS E.
  Fie! now you run this humor out of breath.
  Come, where's the chain? I pray you, let me see it.

SECOND MERCHANT
  My business cannot brook this dalliance.   59
  Good sir, say whe'r you'll answer me or no.   60
  If not, I'll leave him to the officer.

ANTIPHOLUS E.
  I answer you! What should I answer you?

ANGELO
  The money that you owe me for the chain.

ANTIPHOLUS E.
  I owe you none till I receive the chain.

ANGELO
  You know I gave it you half an hour since.

---

48 *dalliance* idle delay   56 *send . . . token* give me a token (e.g., the Courtesan's ring) showing my right to it   59 *brook* endure

ANTIPHOLUS E.
  You gave me none; you wrong me much to say so.

ANGELO
  You wrong me more, sir, in denying it.
68 Consider how it stands upon my credit.

SECOND MERCHANT
  Well, officer, arrest him at my suit.

OFFICER
70 I do; and charge you in the duke's name to obey me.

ANGELO
  This touches me in reputation.
  Either consent to pay this sum for me,
  Or I attach you by this officer.

ANTIPHOLUS E.
  Consent to pay thee that I never had!
  Arrest me, foolish fellow, if thou dar'st.

ANGELO
  Here is thy fee; arrest him, officer.
  I would not spare my brother in this case,
78 If he should scorn me so apparently.

OFFICER
  I do arrest you, sir; you hear the suit.

ANTIPHOLUS E.
80 I do obey thee till I give thee bail.
  But, sirrah, you shall buy this sport as dear
  As all the metal in your shop will answer.

ANGELO
  Sir, sir, I shall have law in Ephesus,
  To your notorious shame, I doubt it not.
    Enter Dromio [of] Syracuse from the bay.

DROMIO S.
  Master, there's a bark of Epidamnum
  That stays but till her owner comes aboard,
87 And then she bears away. Our fraughtage, sir,

---

68 *how   credit* how my credit (both my solvency and my integrity) is involved **78** *apparently* openly **87** *fraughtage* baggage

I have conveyed aboard, and I have bought
The oil, the balsamum, and aqua vitae.   89
The ship is in her trim; the merry wind   90
Blows fair from land; they stay for nought at all
But for their owner, master, and yourself.

ANTIPHOLUS E.

How now, a madman? Why, thou peevish sheep,   93
What ship of Epidamnum stays for me?

DROMIO S.

A ship you sent me to, to hire waftage.   95

ANTIPHOLUS E.

Thou drunken slave, I sent thee for a rope,
And told thee to what purpose, and what end.

DROMIO S.

You sent me for a rope's end as soon.   98
You sent me to the bay, sir, for a bark.

ANTIPHOLUS E.

I will debate this matter at more leisure,   100
And teach your ears to list me with more heed.
To Adriana, villain, hie thee straight.
Give her this key, and tell her, in the desk
That's covered o'er with Turkish tapestry,
There is a purse of ducats; let her send it.
Tell her I am arrested in the street,
And that shall bail me. Hie thee, slave, be gone!
On, officer, to prison till it come.

                 Exeunt [all but Dromio of Syracuse].

DROMIO S.

To Adriana – that is where we dined,
Where Dowsabel did claim me for her husband.   110
She is too big, I hope, for me to compass.

---

89 *balsamum* balm; *aqua vitae* spirits   90 *in her trim* rigged and ready   93–94 *sheep . . . ship* (pronounced similarly; a favorite Elizabethan pun)   95 *waftage* passage by sea   98 *You . . . soon* i.e., you just as likely sent me (for a rope's end) to be hanged   110 *Dowsabel* i.e., Gentle and Beautiful (from French *douce et belle*), perhaps with a pun on "douse," to beat, extinguish (as in a fire), or immerse in water

Thither I must, although against my will,
For servants must their masters' minds fulfill.   *Exit.*

                                    *

∾ **IV.2** *Enter Adriana and Luciana.*

ADRIANA
    Ah, Luciana, did he tempt thee so?
2   Mightst thou perceive austerely in his eye
    That he did plead in earnest? yea or no?
    Looked he or red or pale, or sad or merrily?
    What observation mad'st thou in this case
6   Of his heart's meteors tilting in his face?
LUCIANA
7   First he denied you had in him no right.
ADRIANA
8   He meant he did me none; the more my spite.
LUCIANA
    Then swore he that he was a stranger here.
ADRIANA
10   And true he swore, though yet forsworn he were.
LUCIANA
    Then pleaded I for you.
ADRIANA   And what said he?
LUCIANA
    That love I begged for you he begged of me.
ADRIANA
    With what persuasion did he tempt thy love?
LUCIANA
14   With words that in an honest suit might move.
    First, he did praise my beauty, then my speech.

IV.2 Before the house of Antipholus of Ephesus   **2** *austerely* plainly   **6** *meteors tilting* passions warring   **7** *no* any   **8** *spite* vexation   **14** *honest* virtuous, honorable

ADRIANA
  Didst speak him fair?   16
LUCIANA   Have patience, I beseech.
ADRIANA
  I cannot, nor I will not hold me still;
  My tongue, though not my heart, shall have his will.   18
  He is deformèd, crooked, old and sere,   19
  Ill-faced, worse bodied, shapeless everywhere;   20
  Vicious, ungentle, foolish, blunt, unkind,
  Stigmatical in making, worse in mind.   22
LUCIANA
  Who would be jealous then of such a one?
  No evil lost is wailed when it is gone.
ADRIANA
  Ah, but I think him better than I say,
  And yet would herein others' eyes were worse.
  Far from her nest the lapwing cries away;   27
  My heart prays for him, though my tongue do curse.
    Enter Dromio of Syracuse.
DROMIO S.
  Here, go – the desk, the purse – sweet, now, make
    haste.
LUCIANA
  How hast thou lost thy breath?   30
DROMIO S.   By running fast.
ADRIANA
  Where is thy master, Dromio? Is he well?
DROMIO S.
  No, he's in Tartar limbo, worse than hell.   32
  A devil in an everlasting garment hath him;   33

---

16 *Didst . . . fair* i.e., did you, in turn, speak engagingly to him   18 *his* its
19 *sere* dried up   22 *Stigmatical in making* deformed in body   27 *Far . . .
away* (the lapwing protects her nest by flying about elsewhere)   32 *Tartar
limbo* (Limbo properly is a benign Christian place in hell for unbaptized in-
fants; "Tartar" combines this with a pagan place of punishment)   33 *everlasting garment* the leather, or buff (cf. l. 36), uniform of an Elizabethan
officer of the law

One whose hard heart is buttoned up with steel;
A fiend, a fairy, pitiless and rough;
A wolf, nay worse, a fellow all in buff;

37   A back-friend, a shoulder-clapper, one that counter-
        mands
        The passages of alleys, creeks, and narrow lands;

39   A hound that runs counter and yet draws dry-foot
        well:

40   One that before the judgment carries poor souls to
        hell.

ADRIANA
Why, man, what is the matter?

DROMIO S.

42   I do not know the matter; he is 'rested on the case.

ADRIANA
What, is he arrested? Tell me at whose suit.

DROMIO S.
I know not at whose suit he is arrested well;

45   But a's in a suit of buff which 'rested him, that can I
        tell.

46   Will you send him, mistress, redemption, the money in
        his desk?

ADRIANA
Go fetch it, sister.   *Exit Luciana.*
                      This I wonder at,
That he, unknown to me, should be in debt.

49   Tell me, was he arrested on a band?

---

37 *back-friend* the type of "friend" (police officer) who claps one on the back
or shoulder; *countermands* prohibits   39 *counter* (1) opposite to the direction of the game in a hunt, (2) the name of a debtors' prison; *draws dry-foot*
hunts by the scent of the foot   40 *judgment* (1) legal verdict, (2) day of judgment   42 *'rested on the case* arrested (1) in a lawsuit, (2) by chance, (3) on ap-
pearances, or circumstantial evidence   45 *a's* he's   46 *mistress, redemption*
(possibly should be the Fourth Folio's "Mistress Redemption." This reading
would carry out the idea of "judgment"; and cf. Dromio's *Mistress Satan,*
IV.3.47)   49 *band* bond

DROMIO S.

   Not on a band, but on a stronger thing: *50*

   A chain, a chain. Do you not hear it ring?

ADRIANA

   What, the chain?

DROMIO S.

   No, no, the bell; 'tis time that I were gone.

   It was two ere I left him, and now the clock strikes one.

ADRIANA

   The hours come back! That did I never hear.

DROMIO S.

   O yes; if any hour meet a sergeant, a turns back for *56*

   very fear.

ADRIANA

   As if Time were in debt! How fondly dost thou reason!

DROMIO S.

   Time is a very bankrupt, and owes more than he's worth *58*

   to season.

   Nay, he's a thief too: have you not heard men say,

   That Time comes stealing on by night and day?   *60*

   If a be in debt and theft, and a sergeant in the way,

   Hath he not reason to turn back an hour in a day?

     Enter Luciana.

ADRIANA

   Go, Dromio; there's the money, bear it straight,

   And bring thy master home immediately.

                  [Exit Dromio of Syracuse.]

   Come, sister; I am pressed down with conceit –   *65*

   Conceit, my comfort and my injury.

                   Exit [with Luciana].

          *

---

56 *hour* (pun on similarly pronounced "whore"); *a* it, she (also "he") **58**
owes . . . season (some obscure jest is intended: "season" may have several
meanings, including "the opportunity") **65** *conceit* thought

∾ **IV.3** *Enter Antipholus of Syracuse.*

ANTIPHOLUS S.
There's not a man I meet but doth salute me
As if I were their well-acquainted friend;
And everyone doth call me by my name.
Some tender money to me; some invite me;
Some other give me thanks for kindnesses;
Some offer me commodities to buy.
Even now a tailor called me in his shop
And showed me silks that he had bought for me,
And therewithal took measure of my body.
10   Sure, these are but imaginary wiles,
11   And Lapland sorcerers inhabit here.
    Enter Dromio [of] Syracuse.
DROMIO S. Master, here's the gold you sent me for.
13   What, have you got the picture of old Adam new appareled?
ANTIPHOLUS S.
What gold is this? What Adam dost thou mean?
DROMIO S. Not that Adam that kept the Paradise, but
that Adam that keeps the prison; he that goes in the
18   calf's skin that was killed for the Prodigal; he that came
behind you, sir, like an evil angel, and bid you forsake
20   your liberty.
ANTIPHOLUS S. I understand thee not.
DROMIO S. No? why, 'tis a plain case: he that went, like a
bass viol, in a case of leather; the man, sir, that when

IV.3 The **mart** **10** *imaginary wiles* tricks of the imagination **11** *Lapland* (famous for sorcery) **13–14** *What . . . appareled* (Is the sergeant of law off on other business? Perhaps Dromio is asking if Antipholus has obtained the sergeant a new "suit," as in both legal case and apparel.) **18** *calf's skin , , , Prodigal* (Allusion to the fatted calf killed for the Prodigal Son. This running joke about the leather-clad sergeant persists through *case of leather*, l. 23.)

gentlemen are tired gives them a sob, and 'rests them; 24
he, sir, that takes pity on decayed men and gives them
suits of durance; he that sets up his rest to do more ex- 26
ploits with his mace than a morris pike. 27

ANTIPHOLUS S.   What, thou mean'st an officer?

DROMIO S.   Ay, sir, the sergeant of the band; he that
brings any man to answer it that breaks his band; one 30
that thinks a man always going to bed, and says, "God
give you good rest!"

ANTIPHOLUS S.   Well, sir, there rest in your foolery. Is
there any ship puts forth tonight? May we be gone?

DROMIO S.   Why, sir, I brought you word an hour since
that the bark *Expedition* put forth tonight; and then
were you hindered by the sergeant to tarry for the hoy 37
Delay. Here are the angels that you sent for to deliver 38
you.

ANTIPHOLUS S.
The fellow is distract, and so am I; 40
And here we wander in illusions.
Some blessèd power deliver us from hence!
    Enter a Courtesan.

COURTESAN
Well met, well met, Master Antipholus.
I see, sir, you have found the goldsmith now.
Is that the chain you promised me today?

ANTIPHOLUS S.
Satan, avoid! I charge thee tempt me not! 46

DROMIO S.   Master, is this Mistress Satan?

ANTIPHOLUS S.   It is the devil.

---

24 *sob* a rest, or breather, for horses   26 *suits of durance* clothes that last long
(but Dromio, tireless punner, means also long-lasting legal suits – then very
common – or cases that end in prison); *sets . . . rest* plays with all he has, with
a pun on (ar)rest   27 *mace* official staff of the sergeant; *morris pike* Moorish
pike   37 *hoy* small coasting vessel   38 *angels* coins worth about 50p. apiece
(but there are theological overtones)   46 *avoid* be gone

49 DROMIO S.   Nay, she is worse; she is the devil's dam. And
50 here she comes in the habit of a light wench, and
    thereof comes that the wenches say, "God damn me";
    that's as much as to say, "God make me a light wench."
    It is written, they appear to men like angels of light;
54 light is an effect of fire, and fire will burn; ergo, light
55 wenches will burn. Come not near her.

COURTESAN
    Your man and you are marvelous merry, sir.
57 Will you go with me? We'll mend our dinner here.

58 DROMIO S.   Master, if you do, expect spoon meat, or be-
    speak a long spoon.

60 ANTIPHOLUS S.   Why, Dromio?

61 DROMIO S.   Marry, he must have a long spoon that must
    eat with the devil.

ANTIPHOLUS S.
    Avoid then, fiend! What tell'st thou me of supping?
    Thou art, as you are all, a sorceress.
    I conjure thee to leave me and be gone.

COURTESAN
    Give me the ring of mine you had at dinner,
    Or, for my diamond, the chain you promised,
    And I'll be gone, sir, and not trouble you.

DROMIO S.
69 Some devils ask but the parings of one's nail,
70 A rush, a hair, a drop of blood, a pin,
    A nut, a cherrystone;
    But she, more covetous, would have a chain.

_____
49 *dam* mother   50 *habit* dress; *light* promiscuous   54 *ergo* therefore (con-
cluding a syllogism)   55 *burn* infect you with a sexually transmitted disease
57 *mend* finish (i.e., the courtesan will provide "dessert")   58 *spoon meat* soft
or baby food   61–62 (proverbial; one who eats with the devil will want to
keep his distance)   69–74 *Some . . . it* (Prose in the folio text; hence irregu-
lar lines when set as verse, as here. The meaning through l. 72 is that, though
most witches – cf. l. 77 – require only their intended victims' bodily waste,
such as hair or nail clippings, or cheap possessions in order to cast their
spells, this woman requires an expensive chain.)

Master, be wise; and if you give it her,
The devil will shake her chain and fright us with it.

COURTESAN

I pray you, sir, my ring, or else the chain.
I hope you do not mean to cheat me so?

ANTIPHOLUS S.

Avaunt, thou witch! Come, Dromio, let us go.

DROMIO S.

Fly pride, says the peacock: mistress, that you know.   78

Exit [with Antipholus of Syracuse].

COURTESAN

Now, out of doubt, Antipholus is mad,
Else would he never so demean himself.   80
A ring he hath of mine worth forty ducats,
And for the same he promised me a chain;
Both one and other he denies me now.
The reason that I gather he is mad,
Besides this present instance of his rage,   85
Is a mad tale he told today at dinner,
Of his own doors being shut against his entrance.
Belike his wife, acquainted with his fits,
On purpose shut the doors against his way.
My way is now to hie home to his house,   90
And tell his wife that, being lunatic,
He rushed into my house and took perforce   92
My ring away. This course I fittest choose,
For forty ducats is too much to lose.   *[Exit.]*

*

78 *Fly . . . know* i.e., how strange that the Courtesan should, like the proud
peacock, decry pride (perhaps with play on "pride" in the sense of sexual desire) 80 *demean* behave 85 *rage* wild manner, madness 92 *perforce* by
force

∾ **IV.4** *Enter Antipholus [of] Ephesus, with a Jailer.*

ANTIPHOLUS E.
Fear me not, man; I will not break away.
I'll give thee, ere I leave thee, so much money,
3   To warrant thee, as I am 'rested for.
My wife is in a wayward mood today,
And will not lightly trust the messenger.
6   That I should be attached in Ephesus,
I tell you, 'twill sound harshly in her ears.
Enter Dromio of Ephesus, with a rope's end.
Here comes my man; I think he brings the money.
How now, sir; have you that I sent you for?
DROMIO E.
10   Here's that, I warrant you, will pay them all.
ANTIPHOLUS E.
But where's the money?
DROMIO E.
Why, sir, I gave the money for the rope.
ANTIPHOLUS E.
Five hundred ducats, villain, for a rope?
DROMIO E.
14   I'll serve you, sir, five hundred at the rate.
ANTIPHOLUS E.
To what end did I bid thee hie thee home?
DROMIO E.   To a rope's end, sir; and to that end am I re-
turned.
ANTIPHOLUS E.
And to that end, sir, I will welcome you.
[Beats him.]
OFFICER   Good sir, be patient.

IV.4 A street   **3** *To warrant* as security for   **6** *attached* arrested   **14** *I'll . . . rate* I'll get you five hundred ropes at that price

DROMIO E.   Nay, 'tis for me to be patient; I am in adver- 20
sity.

OFFICER   Good now, hold thy tongue.   22

DROMIO E.   Nay, rather persuade him to hold his hands.

ANTIPHOLUS E.   Thou whoreson, senseless villain!   24

DROMIO E.   I would I were senseless, sir, that I might not
feel your blows.

ANTIPHOLUS E.   Thou art sensible in nothing but blows,   27
and so is an ass.

DROMIO E.   I am an ass indeed; you may prove it by my
long ears. I have served him from the hour of my nativ-   30
ity to this instant, and have nothing at his hands for my
service but blows. When I am cold, he heats me with
beating; when I am warm, he cools me with beating. I
am waked with it when I sleep, raised with it when I sit,
driven out of doors with it when I go from home, wel-
comed home with it when I return; nay, I bear it on my
shoulders, as a beggar wont her brat; and, I think, when 37
he hath lamed me, I shall beg with it from door to
door.

Enter Adriana, Luciana, Courtesan, and a
Schoolmaster, called Pinch.

ANTIPHOLUS E.   Come, go along; my wife is coming   40
yonder.

DROMIO E.   Mistress, *respice finem,* respect your end; or 42
rather, the prophecy like the parrot, "Beware the rope's
end."

ANTIPHOLUS E.   Wilt thou still talk?
Beats Dromio.

COURTESAN
How say you now? Is not your husband mad?

---

22 *Good now* for heaven's sake   24 *whoreson* (the equivalent of "son of a
bitch")   27 *sensible* (1) intelligent, (2) sensitive   30 *ears* (pun on "years";
Dromio is saying that he is a fool for having served so long)   37 *wont* is ac-
customed (to bear)   42 *respice finem* remember (your) end (a pious proverb
sometimes taught to parrots; with this was associated the punning expression
"*respice funem,*" "remember the rope" – or hangman)

ADRIANA
His incivility confirms no less.

48 Good Doctor Pinch, you are a conjurer;
Establish him in his true sense again,

50 And I will please you what you will demand.

LUCIANA
51 Alas, how fiery and how sharp he looks!

COURTESAN
52 Mark how he trembles in his ecstasy!

PINCH
Give me your hand and let me feel your pulse.

ANTIPHOLUS E.
There is my hand, and let it feel your ear.
    [Strikes him.]

PINCH
I charge thee, Satan, housed within this man,
To yield possession to my holy prayers,
And to thy state of darkness hie thee straight.
I conjure thee by all the saints in heaven.

ANTIPHOLUS E.
Peace, doting wizard, peace! I am not mad.

ADRIANA
60 O that thou wert not, poor distressèd soul!

ANTIPHOLUS E.
61 You minion, you, are these your customers?

62 Did this companion with the saffron face
Revel and feast it at my house today,
Whilst upon me the guilty doors were shut
And I denied to enter in my house?

ADRIANA
O husband, God doth know you dined at home;

---

48 *you . . . conjurer* i.e., you can expel evil spirits (as he tries to do, ll. 55–58)
50 *please . . . demand* pay what you ask   51 *sharp* on edge   52 *ecstasy* madness, possession   61 *customers* paying visitors   62 *companion* fellow; *saffron* yellow

Where would you had remained until this time,
Free from these slanders and this open shame!
ANTIPHOLUS E.
Dined at home! Thou villain, what sayest thou?
DROMIO E.
Sir, sooth to say, you did not dine at home.   70
ANTIPHOLUS E.
Were not my doors locked up and I shut out?
DROMIO E.
Perdy, your doors were locked and you shut out.   72
ANTIPHOLUS E.
And did not she herself revile me there?
DROMIO E.
Sans fable, she herself reviled you there.   74
ANTIPHOLUS E.
Did not her kitchen maid rail, taunt, and scorn me?
DROMIO E.
Certes, she did; the kitchen vestal scorned you.   76
ANTIPHOLUS E.
And did not I in rage depart from thence?
DROMIO E.
In verity you did; my bones bear witness,
That since have felt the vigor of his rage.
ADRIANA
Is't good to soothe him in these contraries?   80
PINCH
It is no shame: the fellow finds his vein,
And yielding to him, humors well his frenzy.
ANTIPHOLUS E.
Thou hast suborned the goldsmith to arrest me.   83

---

72 *Perdy* by God (*par Dieu*)   74 *Sans fable* without lying, "no fooling"   76
Certes certainly; *kitchen vestal* (her job, according to Dr. Johnson, was like
that of the vestal virgins of ancient Rome, to keep the fire burning)   80
soothe humor (cf. l. 82); *contraries* perversities, forms of opposition   83
suborned bribed, solicited

ADRIANA

Alas! I sent you money to redeem you,

By Dromio here, who came in haste for it.

DROMIO E.

Money by me! Heart and good will you might;

87 But surely, master, not a rag of money.

ANTIPHOLUS E.

Went'st not thou to her for a purse of ducats?

ADRIANA

He came to me, and I delivered it.

LUCIANA

90 And I am witness with her that she did.

DROMIO E.

God and the ropemaker bear me witness

That I was sent for nothing but a rope!

PINCH

Mistress, both man and master is possessed;

I know it by their pale and deadly looks.

95 They must be bound and laid in some dark room.

ANTIPHOLUS E.

Say, wherefore didst thou lock me forth today?

And why dost thou deny the bag of gold?

ADRIANA

I did not, gentle husband, lock thee forth.

DROMIO E.

And, gentle master, I received no gold;

100 But I confess, sir, that we were locked out.

ADRIANA

Dissembling villain! thou speak'st false in both.

ANTIPHOLUS E.

102 Dissembling harlot! thou art false in all,

103 And art confederate with a damnèd pack

---

87 *rag* (cant term for farthing; also money worn thin) **95** *bound . . . room*
(common treatment for madness) **102** *harlot* (this insult, like most leveled
at women in this period, focuses on sexual conduct, as would "whore," but
works as an all-purpose insult) **103** *confederate* allied

To make a loathsome abject scorn of me;
But with these nails I'll pluck out these false eyes
That would behold in me this shameful sport.
Enter three or four, and offer to bind him. He strives.

ADRIANA
O, bind him, bind him! Let him not come near me.

PINCH
More company! The fiend is strong within him.

LUCIANA
Ay me, poor man, how pale and wan he looks!

ANTIPHOLUS E.
What, will you murder me? Thou jailer, thou,   110
I am thy prisoner; wilt thou suffer them
To make a rescue?

OFFICER   Masters, let him go.
He is my prisoner, and you shall not have him.

PINCH
Go bind this man, for he is frantic too.
[They bind Dromio of Ephesus.]

ADRIANA
What wilt thou do, thou peevish officer?
Hast thou delight to see a wretched man
Do outrage and displeasure to himself?

OFFICER
He is my prisoner; if I let him go,
The debt he owes will be required of me.

ADRIANA
I will discharge thee ere I go from thee.   120
Bear me forthwith unto his creditor,
And, knowing how the debt grows, I will pay it.   122
Good Master Doctor, see him safe conveyed
Home to my house. O most unhappy day!   124

ANTIPHOLUS E.
O most unhappy strumpet!

---

120 *discharge* relieve of responsibility   122 *how . . . grows* the reason for the debt   124 *unhappy* unfortunate, disastrous (stronger than modern usage)

DROMIO E
  Master, I am here entered in bond for you.
ANTIPHOLUS E.
127 Out on thee, villain! Wherefore dost thou mad me?
DROMIO E. Will you be bound for nothing? Be mad,
  good master: cry, "The devil!"
LUCIANA
130 God help, poor souls, how idly do they talk!
ADRIANA
  Go bear him hence. Sister, go you with me.
  Say now, whose suit is he arrested at?
    Exeunt [Pinch and his company with Antipholus and
    Dromio of Ephesus]. Manet Officer, [with] Adriana,
    Luciana, Courtesan.
OFFICER
  One Angelo, a goldsmith; do you know him?
ADRIANA
  I know the man. What is the sum he owes?
OFFICER
135 Two hundred ducats.
ADRIANA   Say, how grows it due!
OFFICER
  Due for a chain your husband had of him.
ADRIANA
  He did bespeak a chain for me, but had it not.
COURTESAN
  When as your husband all in rage today
  Came to my house, and took away my ring –
140 The ring I saw upon his finger now –
  Straight after did I meet him with a chain.
ADRIANA
  It may be so, but I did never see it.
  Come, jailer, bring me where the goldsmith is;
  I long to know the truth hereof at large.

---

127 *mad* madden   130 *idly* senselessly   135 *grows* comes

Enter Antipholus of Syracuse with his rapier drawn,
and Dromio of Syracuse.

LUCIANA

God, for thy mercy! They are loose again.

ADRIANA

And come with naked swords.   146
Let's call more help to have them bound again.   147

Run all out.

OFFICER   Away! they'll kill us.

Exeunt omnes, as fast as may be, frighted.

ANTIPHOLUS S.

I see these witches are afraid of swords.

DROMIO S.

She that would be your wife now ran from you.   150

ANTIPHOLUS S.

Come to the Centaur; fetch our stuff from thence.
I long that we were safe and sound aboard.

DROMIO S.   Faith, stay here this night; they will surely do
us no harm; you saw they speak us fair; give us gold.
Methinks they are such a gentle nation that, but for the
mountain of mad flesh that claims marriage of me, I
could find in my heart to stay here still, and turn witch.   157

ANTIPHOLUS S.

I will not stay tonight for all the town;
Therefore away, to get our stuff aboard.   *Exeunt.*

∗

∾ **V.1** *Enter the [Second] Merchant and [Angelo]*
the Goldsmith

ANGELO

I am sorry, sir, that I have hindered you;

---

146 *naked* drawn   **147–48** (The two stage directions of the folio duplicate
each other. Possibly the second was the original direction, and *Run all out*
was written in the margin of the prompt copy.)   **157** *still* always
  V.1 Before a priory

But I protest he **had** the chain of me,
Though most dishonestly he doth deny it.

SECOND MERCHANT
How is the man esteemed here in the city?

ANGELO
Of very reverend reputation, sir,
Of credit infinite, highly beloved,
Second to none that lives here in the city;
8   His word might bear my wealth at any time.

SECOND MERCHANT
9   Speak softly; yonder, as I think, he walks.
      Enter Antipholus and Dromio [of Syracuse] again.

ANGELO
10   'Tis so; and that self chain about his neck
11   Which he forswore most monstrously to have.
Good sir, draw near to me, I'll speak to him.
Signor Antipholus, I wonder much
That you would put me to this shame and trouble;
And not without some scandal to yourself,
16   With circumstance and oaths so to deny
This chain which now you wear so openly.
Beside the charge, the shame, imprisonment,
19   You have done wrong to this my honest friend,
20   Who, but for staying on our controversy,
Had hoisted sail and put to sea today.
This chain you had of me; can you deny it?

ANTIPHOLUS S.
I think I had; I never did deny it.

SECOND MERCHANT
Yes, that you did, sir, and forswore it too.

ANTIPHOLUS S.
Who heard me to deny it or forswear it?

---

8 *His . . . wealth* he could have had all my wealth on the strength of his word
9 s.d. *again* (an indication that the action of "Act V" is continuous with that
of "Act IV")   11 *forswore* denied on oath   16 *circumstance* detailed argu-
ment or attempted proof   19 *honest* honorable

SECOND MERCHANT
　These ears of mine, thou know'st, did hear thee.
　Fie on thee, wretch! 'Tis pity that thou liv'st
　To walk where any honest men resort.
ANTIPHOLUS S.
　Thou art a villain to impeach me thus: 29
　I'll prove mine honor and mine honesty 30
　Against thee presently, if thou dar'st stand. 31
SECOND MERCHANT
　I dare, and do defy thee for a villain. 32
　　They draw. Enter Adriana, Luciana, Courtesan, and
　　others.
ADRIANA
　Hold, hurt him not, for God's sake! He is mad.
　Some get within him, take his sword away. 34
　Bind Dromio too, and bear them to my house.
DROMIO S.
　Run, master, run; for God's sake, take a house! 36
　This is some priory. In, or we are spoiled.
　　　　　Exeunt [Antipholus and Dromio of
　　　　　Syracuse] to the Priory.
　　Enter Lady Abbess.
ABBESS
　Be quiet, people. Wherefore throng you hither?
ADRIANA
　To fetch my poor distracted husband hence.
　Let us come in, that we may bind him fast, 40
　And bear him home for his recovery.
ANGELO
　I knew he was not in his perfect wits.
SECOND MERCHANT
　I am sorry now that I did draw on him.

---

29 *impeach* accuse 31 *presently* at once; *stand* i.e., take your position for fighting 32 *defy* challenge; *villain* base person 34 *within him* inside his guard, up close 36 *take* i.e., take to

ABBESS
>How long hath this possession held the man?

ADRIANA
>This week he hath been heavy, sour, sad,
>And much different from the man he was;
>But till this afternoon his passion
>Ne'er brake into extremity of rage.

ABBESS
>Hath he not lost much wealth by wrack of sea?
50 >Buried some dear friend? Hath not else his eye
51 >Strayed his affection in unlawful love –
>A sin prevailing much in youthful men,
>Who give their eyes the liberty of gazing?
>Which of these sorrows is he subject to?

ADRIANA
>To none of these, except it be the last;
>Namely, some love that drew him oft from home.

ABBESS
57 >You should for that have reprehended him.

ADRIANA
>Why, so I did.

ABBESS   Ay, but not rough enough.

ADRIANA
>As roughly as my modesty would let me.

ABBESS
60 >Haply, in private.

ADRIANA   And in assemblies too.

ABBESS
>Ay, but not enough.

ADRIANA
62 >It was the copy of our conference.
63 >In bed, he slept not for my urging it;
>At board, he fed not for my urging it;
>Alone, it was the subject of my theme;

---

51 *Strayed* led astray   57 *reprehended* reprimanded   60 *Haply* perhaps   62
copy theme   63 *for* because of

In company I often glancèd it.   66
Still did I tell him it was vile and bad.   67

ABBESS
And thereof came it that the man was mad.
The venom clamors of a jealous woman
Poisons more deadly than a mad dog's tooth.   70
It seems his sleeps were hindered by thy railing,
And thereof comes it that his head is light.
Thou say'st his meat was sauced with thy upbraidings;
Unquiet meals make ill digestions;
Thereof the raging fire of fever bred.
And what's a fever but a fit of madness?
Thou sayest his sports were hindered by thy brawls.
Sweet recreation barred, what doth ensue
But moody and dull melancholy,
Kinsman to grim and comfortless despair,   80
And at her heels a huge infectious troop
Of pale distemperatures and foes to life?   82
In food, in sport, and life-preserving rest
To be disturbed, would mad or man or beast.
The consequence is, then, thy jealous fits
Hath scared thy husband from the use of wits.

LUCIANA
She never reprehended him but mildly
When he demeaned himself rough, rude, and wildly.
Why bear you these rebukes and answer not?

ADRIANA
She did betray me to my own reproof.   90
Good people, enter, and lay hold on him.

ABBESS
No, not a creature enters in my house.

ADRIANA
Then let your servants bring my husband forth.

---

66 *glancèd* touched upon   67 *Still* always   82 *distemperatures* disorders   **90**
She . . . reproof she tricked me into testifying against myself

ABBESS

94   Neither: he took this place for sanctuary,
And it shall privilege him from your hands
Till I have brought him to his wits again,
Or lose my labor in assaying it.

ADRIANA

I will attend my husband, be his nurse,
Diet his sickness, for it is my office,
100   And will have no attorney but myself;
And therefore let me have him home with me.

ABBESS

Be patient, for I will not let him stir
Till I have used the approvèd means I have,
With wholesome syrups, drugs, and holy prayers,
105   To make of him a formal man again.
106   It is a branch and parcel of mine oath,
A charitable duty of my order.
Therefore depart and leave him here with me.

ADRIANA

I will not hence and leave my husband here;
110   And ill it doth beseem your holiness
To separate the husband and the wife.

ABBESS

Be quiet, and depart; thou shalt not have him.   *[Exit.]*

LUCIANA

Complain unto the duke of this indignity.

ADRIANA

Come, go. I will fall prostrate at his feet,
And never rise until my tears and prayers
Have won his grace to come in person hither,
And take perforce my husband from the abbess.

SECOND MERCHANT

By this, I think, the dial points at five:

---

94 *sanctuary* (those who sought refuge in churches and other holy places were beyond the reach of the law)   **100** *attorney* agent   **105** *formal* in proper form, sane   **106** *branch and parcel* part and parcel

Anon, I'm sure, the duke himself in person
Comes this way to the melancholy vale,   *120*
The place of death and sorry execution,   *121*
Behind the ditches of the abbey here.

ANGELO
Upon what cause?

SECOND MERCHANT
To see a reverend Syracusian merchant,
Who put unluckily into this bay
Against the laws and statutes of this town,
Beheaded publicly for his offense.

ANGELO
See where they come. We will behold his death.

LUCIANA
Kneel to the duke before he pass the abbey.
 Enter the Duke of Ephesus, and [Egeon] the Merchant
 of Syracuse, bareheaded, with the Headsman, and
 other Officers.

DUKE
Yet once again proclaim it publicly,   *130*
If any friend will pay the sum for him,
He shall not die; so much we tender him.   *132*

ADRIANA
Justice, most sacred duke, against the abbess!

DUKE
She is a virtuous and a reverend lady.
It cannot be that she hath done thee wrong.

ADRIANA
May it please your grace, Antipholus, my husband,
Who I made lord of me and all I had,
At your important letters, this ill day   *138*
A most outrageous fit of madness took him,
That desperately he hurried through the street –   *140*
With him his bondman, all as mad as he –

---

121 *sorry* causing sorrow **132** *tender* grant **138** *important* importunate,
beseeching

Doing displeasure to the citizens
By rushing in their houses, bearing thence
144   Rings, jewels, anything his rage did like.
Once did I get him bound and sent him home,
146   Whilst to take order for the wrongs I went
That here and there his fury had committed.
148   Anon, I wot not by what strong escape,
He broke from those that had the guard of him,
150   And with his mad attendant and himself,
Each one with ireful passion, with drawn swords
Met us again and, madly bent on us,
Chased us away, till, raising of more aid,
We came again to bind them. Then they fled
Into this abbey, whither we pursued them;
And here the abbess shuts the gates on us,
And will not suffer us to fetch him out,
Nor send him forth that we may bear him hence.
Therefore, most gracious duke, with thy command
160   Let him be brought forth and borne hence for help.

DUKE
Long since thy husband served me in my wars,
And I to thee engaged a prince's word,
When thou didst make him master of thy bed,
To do him all the grace and good I could.
Go, some of you, knock at the abbey gate
And bid the Lady Abbess come to me.
I will determine this before I stir.
      Enter a Messenger.

MESSENGER
O mistress, mistress, shift and save yourself!
My master and his man are both broke loose,
170   Beaten the maids a-row and bound the doctor,
Whose beard they have singed off with brands of fire;
And ever as it blazed they threw on him

---

144 *rage* madness   146 *take order* settle   148 *wot* know; *strong* violent   170
a-row one by one (or so that they lie in a row)

Great pails of puddled mire to quench the hair.
My master preaches patience to him, and the while
His man with scissors nicks him like a fool;   175
And sure, unless you send some present help,
Between them they will kill the conjurer.

ADRIANA
Peace, fool! thy master and his man are here,
And that is false thou dost report to us.

MESSENGER
Mistress, upon my life, I tell you true;   180
I have not breathed almost since I did see it.
He cries for you and vows, if he can take you,
To scorch your face and to disfigure you.
    Cry within.
Hark, hark! I hear him, mistress. Fly, be gone!

DUKE
Come, stand by me; fear nothing. Guard with hal-   185
    berds!

ADRIANA
Ay, me, it is my husband! Witness you,
That he is borne about invisible.
Even now we housed him in the abbey here,
And now he's there, past thought of human reason.
    Enter Antipholus [of Ephesus] and Dromio of Ephesus.

ANTIPHOLUS E.
Justice, most gracious duke! O grant me justice,   190
Even for the service that long since I did thee,
When I bestrid thee in the wars and took   192
Deep scars to save thy life; even for the blood
That then I lost for thee, now grant me justice.

EGEON
Unless the fear of death doth make me dote,
I see my son Antipholus and Dromio.

---

175 *nicks . . . fool* cuts his hair to make him look like an Elizabethan fool
185 *halberds* long spears with a blade   192 *bestrid thee* stood over and protected you when you were down

ANTIPHOLUS E.
  Justice, sweet prince, against that woman there!
  She whom thou gav'st to me to be my wife,
  That hath abusèd and dishonored me,
200 Even in the strength and height of injury!
  Beyond imagination is the wrong
  That she this day hath shameless thrown on me.

DUKE
203 Discover how, and thou shalt find me just.

ANTIPHOLUS E.
  This day, great duke, she shut the doors upon me,
205 While she with harlots feasted in my house.

DUKE
  A grievous fault! Say, woman, didst thou so?

ADRIANA
  No, my good lord. Myself, he, and my sister
  Today did dine together. So befall my soul
209 As this is false he burdens me withal!

LUCIANA
210 Ne'er may I look on day, nor sleep on night,
  But she tells to your highness simple truth!

ANGELO
  O perjured woman! They are both forsworn;
  In this the madman justly chargeth them.

ANTIPHOLUS E.
  My liege, I am advisèd what I say,
  Neither disturbed with the effect of wine,
  Nor heady-rash, provoked with raging ire,
  Albeit my wrongs might make one wiser mad.
  This woman locked me out this day from dinner.
219 That goldsmith there, were he not packed with her,
220 Could witness it, for he was with me then;
  Who parted with me to go fetch a chain,

---

200 *in . . . injury* to the most injurious extremes   203 *Discover* reveal   205
harlots vile companions   209 *he . . . withal* with which he charges me   219
packed in conspiracy

Promising to bring it to the Porpentine,
Where Balthasar and I did dine together.
Our dinner done, and he not coming thither,
I went to seek him. In the street I met him,
And in his company that gentleman.
There did this perjured goldsmith swear me down
That I this day of him received the chain,
Which, God he knows, I saw not; for the which
He did arrest me with an officer.   230
I did obey, and sent my peasant home   231
For certain ducats; he with none returned.
Then fairly I bespoke the officer   233
To go in person with me to my house.
By the way we met
My wife, her sister, and a rabble more   236
Of vile confederates. Along with them
They brought one Pinch, a hungry lean-faced villain,
A mere anatomy, a mountebank,   239
A threadbare juggler, and a fortune-teller,   240
A needy, hollow-eyed, sharp-looking wretch,   241
A living dead man. This pernicious slave,
Forsooth, took on him as a conjurer,   243
And gazing in mine eyes, feeling my pulse,
And with no face, as 'twere, outfacing me,
Cries out, I was possessed. Then all together
They fell upon me, bound me, bore me thence,
And in a dark and dankish vault at home
There left me and my man, both bound together,
Till, gnawing with my teeth my bonds in sunder,   250
I gained my freedom, and immediately
Ran hither to your grace; whom I beseech
To give me ample satisfaction
For these deep shames and great indignities.

---

231 *peasant* servant (dismissively); here slave   233 *fairly* politely   236 *rabble* mob   239 *mere* sheer; *anatomy* skeleton; *mountebank* charlatan, quack
241 *sharp* hungry   243 *took . . . as* assumed the role of

ANGELO
    My lord, in truth, thus far I witness with him,
    That he dined not at home, but was locked out.

DUKE
    But had he such a chain of thee, or no?

ANGELO
    He had, my lord; and when he ran in here,
    These people saw the chain about his neck.

SECOND MERCHANT
260   Besides, I will be sworn these ears of mine
    Heard you confess you had the chain of him,
    After you first forswore it on the mart,
    And thereupon I drew my sword on you;
    And then you fled into this abbey here,
    From whence, I think, you are come by miracle.

ANTIPHOLUS E.
    I never came within these abbey walls,
    Nor ever didst thou draw thy sword on me.
    I never saw the chain, so help me heaven!
    And this is false you burden me withal.

DUKE
270   Why, what an intricate impeach is this!
271   I think you all have drunk of Circe's cup.
    If here you housed him, here he would have been.
273   If he were mad, he would not plead so coldly.
    You say he dined at home; the goldsmith here
    Denies that saying. Sirrah, what say you?

DROMIO E.
    Sir, he dined with her there, at the Porpentine.

COURTESAN
    He did, and from my finger snatched that ring.

ANTIPHOLUS E.
    'Tis true, my liege; this ring I had of her.

---

270 *intricate impeach* involved accusation   271 *Circe's cup* (the enchantress's drink turned men into animals)   273 *coldly* reasonably

DUKE
  Saw'st thou him enter at the abbey here?
COURTESAN
  As sure, my liege, as I do see your grace.   280
DUKE
  Why, this is strange. Go call the abbess hither.
  I think you are all mated or stark mad.   282
                              Exit one to the Abbess.
EGEON
  Most mighty duke, vouchsafe me speak a word.
  Haply I see a friend will save my life,
  And pay the sum that may deliver me.
DUKE
  Speak freely, Syracusian, what thou wilt.
EGEON
  Is not your name, sir, called Antipholus?
  And is not that your bondman Dromio?
DROMIO E.
  Within this hour I was his bondman, sir;
  But he, I thank him, gnawed in two my cords.   290
  Now am I Dromio, and his man, unbound.
EGEON
  I am sure you both of you remember me.
DROMIO E.
  Ourselves we do remember, sir, by you;
  For lately we were bound, as you are now.
  You are not Pinch's patient, are you, sir?   295
EGEON
  Why look you strange on me? You know me well.
ANTIPHOLUS E.
  I never saw you in my life till now.
EGEON
  Oh, grief hath changed me since you saw me last,

---

282 *mated* stupefied   295 *Pinch's patient* i.e., bound as Dromio had been
while undergoing "treatment" for madness

299   And careful hours, with Time's deformèd hand,
300   Have written strange defeatures in my face.
        But tell me yet, dost thou not know my voice?

ANTIPHOLUS E.   Neither.

EGEON   Dromio, nor thou?

DROMIO E.   No, trust me, sir, not I.

EGEON   I am sure thou dost.

DROMIO E.   Ay, sir, but I am sure I do not; and whatso-
ever a man denies, you are now bound to believe him.

EGEON
        Not know my voice! O Time's extremity,
        Hast thou so cracked and splitted my poor tongue
310   In seven short years, that here my only son
        Knows not my feeble key of untuned cares?
312   Though now this grainèd face of mine be hid
313   In sap-consuming winter's drizzled snow,
        And all the conduits of my blood froze up,
        Yet hath my night of life some memory,
        My wasting lamps some fading glimmer left,
317   My dull deaf ears a little use to hear.
        All these old witnesses – I cannot err –
        Tell me thou art my son Antipholus.

320 ANTIPHOLUS E.
        I never saw my father in my life.

EGEON
        But seven years since, in Syracusa, boy,
        Thou know'st we parted; but perhaps, my son,
        Thou sham'st to acknowledge me in misery.

ANTIPHOLUS E.
        The duke and all that know me in the city

---

299 *careful* full of care   300 *defeatures* disfigurements   312 *my . . . cares* my
voice made feeble by discordant cares (the image is the favorite Elizabethan
one of life losing its harmony)   313 *grainèd* furrowed   317 *wasting lamps*
dimming eyes

Can witness with me that it is not so.
I ne'er saw Syracusa in my life.

DUKE

I tell thee, Syracusian, twenty years
Have I been patron to Antipholus,
During which time he ne'er saw Syracusa.   330
I see thy age and dangers make thee dote.
    Enter the Abbess, with Antipholus of Syracuse and
    Dromio of Syracuse.

ABBESS

Most mighty duke, behold a man much wronged.
    All gather to see them.

ADRIANA

I see two husbands, or mine eyes deceive me!

DUKE

One of these men is genius to the other;   334
And so of these, which is the natural man,
And which the spirit? Who deciphers them?

DROMIO S.

I, sir, am Dromio; command him away.

DROMIO E.

I, sir, am Dromio; pray let me stay.

ANTIPHOLUS S.

Egeon art thou not? or else his ghost?

DROMIO S.

O, my old master! Who hath bound him here?   340

ABBESS

Whoever bound him, I will loose his bonds,
And gain a husband by his liberty.
Speak, old Egeon, if thou be'st the man
That hadst a wife once called Emilia,
That bore thee at a burden two fair sons.   345
O, if thou be'st the same Egeon, speak,
And speak unto the same Emilia!

---

334 *genius* attendant spirit (cf. *Julius Caesar*, II.1)   **345** *burden* in a single
birth

EGEON
> If I dream not, thou art Emilia.
> If thou art she, tell me where is that son
350   That floated with thee on the fatal raft?

ABBESS
> By men of Epidamnum he and I
> And the twin Dromio all were taken up;
> But by and by rude fishermen of Corinth
> By force took Dromio and my son from them,
> And me they left with those of Epidamnum.
> What then became of them, I cannot tell;
> I to this fortune that you see me in.

DUKE
358   Why, here begins his morning story right:
359   These two Antipholuses, these two so like,
360   And these two Dromios, one in semblance –
361   Besides her urging of her wreck at sea –
> These are the parents to these children,
> Which accidentally are met together.
> Antipholus, thou cam'st from Corinth first?

ANTIPHOLUS S.
> No, sir, not I; I came from Syracuse.

DUKE
> Stay, stand apart; I know not which is which.

ANTIPHOLUS E.
> I came from Corinth, my most gracious lord –

DROMIO E.
> And I with him.

ANTIPHOLUS E.
> Brought to this town by that most famous warrior,
370   Duke Menaphon, your most renownèd uncle.

358–63 (In the folio these lines follow l. 347; the present arrangement –
almost an inevitable one – is that of the Globe edition, following Capell.)
359 *Antipholuses* (four syllables, the "o" being scarcely heard)   360 *in semblance* seeming, appearing   361 *urging* report

ADRIANA

  Which of you two did dine with me today?

ANTIPHOLUS S.

  I, gentle mistress.

ADRIANA

  And are not you my husband?

ANTIPHOLUS E.

  No; I say nay to that.

ANTIPHOLUS S.

  And so do I; yet did she call me so;

  And this fair gentlewoman, her sister here,

  Did call me brother. *[To Luciana]* What I told you then,

  I hope I shall have leisure to make good,

  If this be not a dream I see and hear.

ANGELO

  That is the chain, sir, which you had of me.   *380*

ANTIPHOLUS S.

  I think it be, sir; I deny it not.

ANTIPHOLUS E.

  And you, sir, for this chain arrested me.

ANGELO

  I think I did, sir; I deny it not.

ADRIANA

  I sent you money, sir, to be your bail,

  By Dromio; but I think he brought it not.

DROMIO E.

  No, none by me.

ANTIPHOLUS S.

  This purse of ducats I received from you,

  And Dromio, my man, did bring them me.

  I see we still did meet each other's man,

  And I was ta'en for him, and he for me,   *390*

  And thereupon these errors are arose.

ANTIPHOLUS E.

  These ducats pawn I for my father here.

DUKE
    It shall not need; thy father hath his life.
COURTESAN
    Sir, I must have that diamond from you.
ANTIPHOLUS E.
    There, take it; and much thanks for my good cheer.
ABBESS
    Renownèd duke, vouchsafe to take the pains
    To go with us into the abbey here,
    And hear at large discoursèd all our fortunes;
    And all that are assembled in this place,
400   That by this sympathizèd one day's error
    Have suffered wrong, go keep us company,
    And we shall make full satisfaction.
403   Thirty-three years have I but gone in travail
    Of you, my sons; and till this present hour
    My heavy burden ne'er deliverèd.
    The duke, my husband, and my children both,
407   And you the calendars of their nativity,
408   Go to a gossips' feast, and go with me;
409   After so long grief such Nativity!
DUKE
410   With all my heart I'll gossip at this feast.
        Exeunt [all but] the two Dromios and two Brothers.
DROMIO S.
    Master, shall I fetch your stuff from shipboard?
ANTIPHOLUS E.
    Dromio, what stuff of mine hast thou embarked?
DROMIO S.
413   Your goods that lay at host, sir, in the Centaur.

---

400 *sympathizèd* felt together   403 *Thirty-three* (The chronology is confusing; see also I.1.125 and V.1.322.); *in travail* (as in giving birth)   407 *you . . . nativity* (i.e., the Dromios; see I.2.41)   408 *gossips' feast* christening feast, at which a "gossip," or godparent, is a sponsor   409 *Nativity* (as repeated and capitalized, the word seems to carry the larger significance of a religious festivity)   410 *gossip at* take part in   413 *at host* in charge of the host

ANTIPHOLUS S.

    He speaks to me. I am your master, Dromio.

    Come, go with us; we'll look to that anon.

    Embrace thy brother there; rejoice with him.

                        Exit [with his Brother].

DROMIO S.

    There is a fat friend at your master's house,

    That kitchened me for you today at dinner;   418

    She now shall be my sister, not my wife.

DROMIO E.

    Methinks you are my glass, and not my brother.   420

    I see by you I am a sweet-faced youth.

    Will you walk in to see their gossiping?

DROMIO S.   Not I, sir; you are my elder.

DROMIO E.   That's a question; how shall we try it?

DROMIO S.   We'll draw cuts for the senior; till then lead 425
    thou first.

DROMIO E.   Nay, then, thus:

    We came into the world like brother and brother;

    And now let's go hand in hand, not one before

    another.   *Exeunt.*

---

418 *kitchened* entertained in the kitchen   **425** *draw cuts* draw straws

FOR THE BEST IN PAPERBACKS, LOOK FOR THE

The distinguished Pelican Shakespeare series, newly revised to be the premier choice for students, professors, and general readers well into the 21st century

NOW AVAILABLE

Antony and Cleopatra
ISBN 0-14-071452-9

The Comedy of Errors
ISBN 0-14-071474-X

Coriolanus
ISBN 0-14-071473-1

Cymbeline
ISBN 0-14-071472-3

Henry IV, Part I
ISBN 0-14-071456-1

Henry IV, Part 2
ISBN 0-14-071457-X

Henry V
ISBN 0-14-071458-8

King Lear
ISBN 0-14-071476-6

King Lear
(The Quarto and Folio Texts)
ISBN 0-14-071490-1

Macbeth
ISBN 0-14-071478-2

Much Ado About Nothing
ISBN 0-14-71480-4

The Narrative Poems
ISBN 0-14-071481-2

Richard III
ISBN 0-14-071483-9

Romeo and Juliet
ISBN 0-14-071484-7

The Tempest
ISBN 0-14-071485-5

Timon of Athens
ISBN 0-14-071487-1

Titus Andronicus
ISBN 0-14-071491-X

Twelfth Night
ISBN 0-14-071489-8

The Two Gentlemen of Verona
ISBN 0-14-071461-8

The Winter's Tale
ISBN 0-14-071488-X

All's Well That Ends Well
ISBN 0-14-071460-X

Measure for Measure
ISBN 0-14-071479-0

As You Like It
ISBN 0-14-071471-5

The Merchant of Venice
ISBN 0-14-071462-6

Hamlet
ISBN 0-14-071454-5

The Merry Wives of Windsor
ISBN 0-14-071464-2

Henry VI, Part 1
ISBN 0-14-071465-0

A Midsummer Night's Dream
ISBN 0-14-071455-3

Henry VI, Part 2
ISBN 0-14-071466-9

Othello
ISBN 0-14-071463-4

Henry VI, Part 3
ISBN 0-14-071467-7

Pericles
ISBN 0-14-071469-3

Henry VIII
ISBN 0-14-071475-8

Richard II
ISBN 0-14-071482-0

Julius Caesar
ISBN 0-14-071468-5

The Sonnets
ISBN 0-14-071453-7

King John
ISBN 0-14-071459-6

The Taming of the Shrew
ISBN 0-14-071451-0

Love's Labor's Lost
ISBN 0-14-071477-4

Troilus and Cressida
ISBN 0-14-071486-3

FOR THE BEST IN PAPERBACKS, LOOK FOR THE

In every corner of the world, on every subject under the sun, Penguin represents quality and variety—the very best in publishing today.

For complete information about books available from Penguin—including Penguin Classics, Penguin Compass, and Puffins—and how to order them, write to us at the appropriate address below. Please note that for copyright reasons the selection of books varies from country to country.

In the United States: Please write to *Penguin Group (USA), P.O. Box 12289 Dept. B, Newark, New Jersey 07101-5289* or call 1-800-788-6262.

In the United Kingdom: Please write to *Dept. EP, Penguin Books Ltd, Bath Road, Harmondsworth, West Drayton, Middlesex UB7 0DA.*

In Canada: Please write to *Penguin Books Canada Ltd, 90 Eglinton Avenue East, Suite 700, Toronto, Ontario M4P 2Y3.*

In Australia: Please write to *Penguin Books Australia Ltd, P.O. Box 257, Ringwood, Victoria 3134.*

In New Zealand: Please write to *Penguin Books (NZ) Ltd, Private Bag 102902, North Shore Mail Centre, Auckland 10.*

In India: Please write to *Penguin Books India Pvt Ltd, 11 Panchsheel Shopping Centre, Panchsheel Park, New Delhi 110 017.*

In the Netherlands: Please write to *Penguin Books Netherlands bv, Postbus 3507, NL-1001 AH Amsterdam.*

In Germany: Please write to *Penguin Books Deutschland GmbH, Metzlerstrasse 26, 60594 Frankfurt am Main.*

In Spain: Please write to *Penguin Books S. A., Bravo Murillo 19, 1° B, 28015 Madrid.*

In Italy: Please write to *Penguin Italia s.r.l., Via Benedetto Croce 2, 20094 Corsico, Milano.*

In France: Please write to *Penguin France, Le Carré Wilson, 62 rue Benjamin Baillaud, 31500 Toulouse.*

In Japan: Please write to *Penguin Books Japan Ltd, Kaneko Building, 2-3-25 Koraku, Bunkyo-Ku, Tokyo 112.*

In South Africa: Please write to *Penguin Books South Africa (Pty) Ltd, Private Bag X14, Parkview, 2122 Johannesburg.*